LIBERTARIANISM
WHAT EVERYONE NEEDS TO KNOW

LIBERTARIANISM

WHAT EVERYONE NEEDS TO KNOW

JASON BRENNAN

OXFORD
UNIVERSITY PRESS

OXFORD
UNIVERSITY PRESS

Oxford University Press is a department of the University of Oxford.
It furthers the University's objective of excellence in research, scholarship,
and education by publishing worldwide.

Oxford   New York
Auckland   Cape Town   Dar es Salaam   Hong Kong   Karachi
Kuala Lumpur   Madrid   Melbourne   Mexico City   Nairobi
New Delhi   Shanghai   Taipei   Toronto

With offices in
Argentina   Austria   Brazil   Chile   Czech Republic   France   Greece
Guatemala   Hungary   Italy   Japan   Poland   Portugal   Singapore
South Korea   Switzerland   Thailand   Turkey   Ukraine   Vietnam

Oxford is a registered trademark of Oxford University Press
in the UK and certain other countries.

Published in the United States of America by
Oxford University Press
198 Madison Avenue, New York, NY 10016

© Oxford University Press 2012

All rights reserved. No part of this publication may be reproduced, stored in a
retrieval system, or transmitted, in any form or by any means, without the prior
permission in writing of Oxford University Press, or as expressly permitted by law,
by license, or under terms agreed with the appropriate reproduction rights organization.
Inquiries concerning reproduction outside the scope of the above should be sent to the
Rights Department, Oxford University Press, at the address above.

You must not circulate this work in any other form
and you must impose this same condition on any acquirer.

Library of Congress Cataloging-in-Publication Data
Brennan, Jason, author.
Libertarianism : what everyone needs to know / Jason Brennan.
pages cm
Includes bibliographical references and index.
ISBN 978–0–19–993391–4 (pbk.) — ISBN 978–0–19–993389–1 (hardback)
1. Libertarianism—United States.   2. United States—Politics and
government.   I. Title.
JC599.U5B675 2012
320.51'2—dc23
2012020049

ISBN 978–0–19–993391–4
ISBN 978–0–19–993389–1

1 3 5 7 9 8 6 4 2
Printed in the United States of America
on acid-free paper

CONTENTS

5 Civil Rights 81

6 Economic Freedom   105

7 Social Justice and the Poor   129

8 Contemporary Problems   150

9 Politics: Yesterday, Today, and Tomorrow   172

INTRODUCTION

Libertarians believe that so long as we do not violate others' rights, we should each be free to live as we choose. To respect one another as equal human beings, we must not force people to serve society, each other, or even themselves.

Critics of libertarianism worry that allowing people so much freedom would produce bad consequences. Critics say, sure, *some* freedom is good, but we also need to guarantee good results. We need government to guarantee good culture, scientific progress, and economic prosperity.

Libertarians agree that freedom does not *guarantee* good results. If people are free to choose for themselves, many will make bad choices. Still, libertarians say, *nothing* guarantees good results, so guarantees are beside the point. Liberty may not guarantee good results, but as a matter of fact it delivers good results.

These are intriguing ideas, whether they are true or false.

I first encountered libertarian ideas in a high school economics class. My teacher, Mr. Lee, suggested I read Henry Hazlitt's *Economics in One Lesson*. It transformed me.

Hazlitt taught me that when evaluating policies, you must see past people's good intentions and look instead at results. He taught me to view politics without romance.

Hazlitt's one lesson is simple. When assessing a proposed policy, he says, do not just examine its immediate effects on the intended beneficiaries. Instead, he advises us, examine both its short-term and long-term consequences on all affected groups.

Hazlitt's lesson is itself a modern version of Frédéric Bastiat's "What Is Seen and What Is Not Seen." Bastiat condenses political economy to one lesson as well. He says:

> There is only one difference between a bad economist and a good one: the bad economist confines himself to the *visible* effect; the good economist takes into account both the effect that can be the seen and those effects that must be foreseen.

This advice is simple and obvious, and yet hardly any of us follow it.

For instance, suppose the once-proud widget industry is failing. The once-mighty General Widgets loses millions of dollars every year it remains in business. Suppose a well-meaning senator proposes that, in order to save General Widget workers' jobs, the government should subsidize General Widgets. Good idea? Hazlitt and Bastiat would advise us to ask where the subsidy money will come from. Subsidies are paid for by taxes. In order to save jobs at General Widgets, we need to take money away from other parts of the economy. Subsidizing General Widgets means transferring resources from the productive part of the economy to the unproductive part of the economy. Subsidizing General Widgets means transferring resources from the wealth-creating to the wealth-destroying part of the economy. When we subsidize General Widgets, we see all the jobs we save on the widget factory floor. We don't see or don't notice all the jobs we destroyed in the rest of the economy, jobs that—because they didn't need to be subsidized—were actually creating value for others.

Libertarians are sometimes thought to have excess enthusiasm for the free market. Sure, critics say, markets tend to work pretty well, and markets tend to deliver the goods. But, critics add, markets also fail or make mistakes. When they fail, this calls for government intervention.

Libertarians say, yes, of course, markets can fail. And, they add, so too can governments fail. It's one thing to argue that in principle, a fully informed and well-motivated government could correct a market failure. It's another thing to argue that a real-life government will actually correct a market failure. When introductory economics textbooks call for government intervention, they stipulate that the governments in question know how to correct market failures and will use their power to do so. In the real world, we don't get to stipulate that governments are like that. That makes all the difference in what we want real-life governments to do.

We might say that unthinking libertarians advocate market solutions without taking into account market failures. Unthinking interventionists advocate government solutions without taking into account government failures. If I had to summarize economic libertarianism in one lesson, it would be this: When assessing different policies, consider both market and government failures. Any person who fails to do so arrives at her political beliefs in an irresponsible way.

The Nobel laureate economist Gary Becker argues that once we take into account both market and government failures, we will rarely advocate government intervention into the market. Just because an ideal government could correct the mistakes of a market doesn't mean that a real government will. Governments make things worse more often than they make things better, Becker says. Now, perhaps Becker is wrong. Perhaps a proper assessment of market and government failures calls for massive government intervention, or even socialism. We could debate that. However, if we're having that debate, we are at least debating politics in an intellectually responsible way. That's an improvement.

Libertarianism is most famous for its view on economics; however, it is not just about economics. It is not even primarily about economics. Libertarian attitudes toward the free market are just an extension of the attitudes toward the rest of social life.

Because libertarianism is not just or even primarily about economics, I do not focus on economic questions until chapter six. Chapter one offers an introduction to libertarian ideas and explains how libertarianism is not really a conservative or a liberal view, at least given how we use those terms in popular debates. (In philosophical language, libertarianism is a species of liberalism, but philosophers mean something different by "liberal" from what Rush Limbaugh means.) Chapter two explains how libertarians think about liberty and gives a general overview of why they think liberty matters. Chapter three investigates issues about personal morality and ethics. It is largely meant to correct mistakes about libertarianism, in particular, the mistake of thinking that most libertarians are followers of Ayn Rand. Chapter four outlines libertarian views about government and democracy. It explains the concept of government failure and explains, in broad terms, why libertarians tend to oppose trying to have government solve problems. Chapter five explains libertarian views about civil liberties, including such hot issues as the War on Drugs, organ sales, and gun control. (I leave some other, hotter issues to chapter eight, on contemporary problems.) Chapter six explains why libertarians support strong property rights, free trade, and the free market. Chapter seven explains libertarian views of social justice. Contrary to a popular misconception, most libertarians throughout history have advocated libertarianism in part out of concern for the poor. Chapter eight addresses some contemporary problems, the kinds of issues debated in talk shows and news broadcasts right now. Finally, chapter nine places libertarianism within contemporary politics. It asks which states and countries are the least and most libertarian. (You may be surprised, but the United States is not the most libertarian country.) It also examines some trends, such as whether the United States and the world are becoming more or less libertarian.

This book is centered on American politics. Though the United States is not the most libertarian country (see question 98), it is the country with the most expressed interest in libertarian ideas. This book is also being published in the middle of an election where, thanks to the Tea Party and to Ron Paul, certain libertarian ideas are in the forefront of politics.

There are many ways to read this book. You could read it straight through, from beginning to end. However, like other books in Oxford University Press's *What Everyone Needs to Know* series, I do not assume readers will do so. Instead, you could start on any question you like. You will also sometimes see certain ideas repeated in different questions, because I do not assume readers started on page 1.

If you are interested primarily in questions about economic liberty, you might start with questions 36 and 37 and then read chapters six, seven, and eight.

If you are interested in libertarians' attitudes toward the weak and oppressed, you might start with chapter seven, then read chapters four, five, six, and eight.

If you are most interested in contemporary political debates, you might start with chapter one, then read chapters eight and nine, and then later return to the other chapters, and in particular, questions 48–50 and 54–61.

If you are most interested in more abstract philosophical questions about the good and right, you might start with chapter one, then read chapters two and three.

Ask yourself, do you think libertarians are selfish ethical egoists who are indifferent to community and to the suffering of the poor, and who just want to protect big business? To correct your misconceptions, I recommend you start with chapter three; then read questions 36, 37, and 71; then chapter seven; and finally question 92.

Thanks to David McBride, my editor at Oxford University Press, for suggesting this book and encouraging me to write it. Thanks to two anonymous referees for valuable feedback on how to shape the book. Thanks to Bryan Caplan, John Hasnas, Alexander McCobin, David Schmidtz, John Thrasher, and Kevin Vallier for helpful discussions of these issues while I was writing. Thanks especially to John Tomasi, my former colleague when I was at Brown. John and I spent years together discussing and formulating an alternative, more humane vision of classical liberalism.

—Jason Brennan
Washington, DC
April 2012

LIBERTARIANISM

WHAT EVERYONE NEEDS TO KNOW

1

THE BASICS OF LIBERTARIANISM

1. What is libertarianism?

Libertarianism is a political philosophy. Libertarians believe respect for individual liberty is the central requirement of justice. They believe human relationships should be based on mutual consent. Libertarians advocate a free society of cooperation, tolerance, and mutual respect.

Libertarianism holds that we should each be permitted to choose how our lives will go, so long as we do not violate others' rights. We do not have to get society's permission to go about our lives. We are not required to answer to or justify ourselves to others. We may not be forced to serve strangers. We may not even be forced to serve *ourselves*—no one may force us to promote our own good. Libertarians believe each of us possesses an inviolability, founded on justice, that forbids others from sacrificing us for the sake of greater social stability, economic efficiency, or better culture. Over our own lives, each of us is sovereign. We are not to be treated like slaves, servants, or helpless children.

Libertarianism is not the most popular political philosophy in the United States. (See questions 12 and 94.) Yet, it derives from commonsense moral thinking. Most Americans agree, in the abstract, that we should be free to do as we please, provided we do not hurt others or violate their rights. Most agree that human relationships should be voluntary. For example, most agree that it would be wrong for me to force you to join my church or book club. Most agree that we should not sacrifice individual people "for the greater good." Most agree it is wrong to force another adult to do something "for her own good."

However, most people think there are many exceptions to these commonsense principles. Libertarians do not. For instance, conservatives want the government to forbid people from exchanging sex for money. Libertarians do not. Many left-liberals want the government to forbid people from hiring undocumented immigrants as nannies. Libertarians do not. Marxists want the government to forbid individuals from owning factories. Libertarians do not.

Libertarians say that if we take seriously the idea that human relationships should be voluntary, then the role of government must be greatly constrained. Many things governments do, and that people want governments to do, cannot be done without treating our neighbors like slaves, servants, or helpless children. From the libertarian standpoint, those who hold other political ideologies, including left-liberals, conservatives, Marxists, fascists, and social democrats, all agree that we should sometimes treat our neighbors like slaves, servants, or children. They just disagree about how and when.

Libertarians tend to distrust government. In part, this is because they believe governments are often incompetent. Society and the market are like ecosystems, and like ecosystems, they are impossible to manage without producing unintended consequences. Governments thus tend to make problems worse, not better. Libertarians also worry that the promise of power tends to attract those who want to exploit others at least as often as it attracts those who want to help.

Libertarianism is not one uniform philosophy, but rather a family of related philosophies. (See question 5.) There is a lot of diversity inside libertarian thought, just as there is diversity inside most other political philosophies. Libertarians share a common core of principles. They sometimes disagree on how to understand these principles. They may think there are some exceptions to these principles, or they may not.

2. What do libertarians advocate?

Libertarians advocate *radical tolerance*. Libertarianism is a demanding doctrine—it demands that we mind our own business, even though most of us would rather not. In a free society, some will choose to follow traditional lifestyles. Others will choose new ways of living. Some will choose tight-knit communities. Some will choose communes. Some will choose a life alone. Some will be wicked. Some will be virtuous. So long as a person lives in peace and respects others' liberty, she may live her life as she chooses. Libertarians say, "Live and let live." No one should be forced to fit anyone else's vision of the good life. Even when we see others leading wicked, imprudent, self-destructive, or stupid lives, we must let them be, so long as those people respect the rights of others. We may try to persuade others to change their ways. We may set good examples. But we may not force them to do better.

Libertarians advocate *radical voluntarism*. Libertarians want all human interactions to be based on consent, not force. Each person should be sovereign over her own life.

Libertarians advocate *radical respect*. Every normal adult has the power to develop and act upon conception of the good life and a plan to realize that conception. People are agents of their own lives. This agency matters—it's what sets humans apart from other sentient creatures. To respect individuals as agents, we must grant them as extensive a sphere of personal, civil, and economic liberty as possible, consistent with others having an equal sphere of liberty.

Libertarians advocate *radical equality*. No people or group of people has any special authority over others. No one rules by right. Every person, regardless of ability, virtue, or social class, has fundamentally the same moral standing. We are all equally sovereign over ourselves and equally nonsovereign over others.

Libertarians advocate *radical peace*. Many people seem to believe that governments may treat the citizens of other countries as if they were not fully human. Libertarians believe every person, no matter where she is born, has the same fundamental moral standing. No nation may sacrifice the interests of foreigners to advance its own economy. Empire and conquest are never justified. Governments may not make war just to secure advantages for own their citizens. Governments may make war only in genuine self-defense.

Libertarians advocate *responsibility*. In a free society, people must take responsibility for their own decisions. They must not externalize the cost of their bad decisions onto others. Libertarians also believe a responsible and free people will band together to solve problems.

Thus, libertarians advocate *radical freedom*. Each person may decide how her life will go. We need not justify ourselves to others. Each of us possesses an inviolability, founded on justice, that forbids others from sacrificing us to achieve greater social stability, economic efficiency, or desirable cultural ends.

3. What do libertarians oppose?

Libertarians reject the idea that society has a good of its own, apart from the individuals within society. They reject the doctrine that individuals are mere cells within a greater social organism.

Libertarians reject the idea that we are born in debt to our neighbors. Our lives are not blank checks to be cashed at society's whim.

Libertarians reject the idea that governments should act like parents toward their citizens. To respect our neighbors, we must let them stand by their own decisions. We must even sometimes let them fall by their own decisions. We must not try to control them, even for their own good. At any rate, "we are doing it for their own good" is often an excuse to do evil.

Libertarians reject the idea that anyone—or any group of people—has any natural authority over anyone else. We are all equally sovereign over ourselves. We are equally nonsovereign over others. The majority has no natural right to rule the minority.

Libertarians reject using violence to achieve goals. Violence is sometimes permissible in self-defense and almost never permissible otherwise. Libertarians do not think governments are exempt from normal moral rules. If it would be wrong for me to force you to do something, then it would normally be wrong for the police to force you to do it.

Libertarians reject the idea that national borders should divide people into insiders and outsiders. They do not think we can forbid each other from moving across these borders, nor can we force people to privilege their fellow citizens.

Libertarians oppose romantic ideas about government. People are people. Handing someone a gun, calling him boss, and charging him with a noble goal will not transform him into a saint. Libertarians are skeptical that those in power will want to use their power to do good. They are also skeptical that those in power will know *how* to do good, even when they want to. If the government were staffed by omniscient angels, many libertarians would accept a larger role for government. However, when governments are staffed by real people with real human flaws, libertarians believe the role of government must be constrained. In our lives, at most, government should set the stage, not be the play.

4. Why do we need to know about libertarianism?

The American public seems to speak with an increasingly libertarian voice. The Tea Party often espouses libertarian-sounding ideas. Recent Gallup polls find that Americans believe the federal government wastes half of every dollar spent. Eighty-two percent of Americans believe the country is badly governed. Sixty-nine percent say they have little or no confidence in Congress. Nearly half believe the government is an immediate threat to citizens' rights and freedoms. Despite high gas prices and the financial crisis, Americans view the gas, banking, and real estate industries more positively than they view their own government.

Of course, distrust of government is not the same as a principled support for libertarian ideals of peace, prosperity, and freedom. Still, in a recent CNN poll, a record high of 63% of Americans said the government does too much and should leave more to individuals and businesses. Fifty percent said that government should not try to promote traditional values. American citizens increasingly seem to favor less extensive government intervention into the economy or social and moral life.

We need to know about libertarianism because the world is becoming more libertarian. In general, across the world, economic barriers are coming down. Tolerance for diversity is increasing. Traditionally unfree countries are becoming freer and freer. We need to ask: Are these developments good or bad? Just how free should everyone become? Should they become as free as libertarians want them to be, or should we limit people's freedom?

We need to know about libertarianism in part because it offers a third way in American politics. American politics has two large camps. The first camp advocates an American police state—one that polices the world at large while also policing its citizens' lifestyles. It advocates having government promote traditional Judeo-Christian virtues. It wants to marginalize or expel alternative modes of life. The second camp advocates an American nanny state—one that tries to nudge and control the behavior of its citizens "for their own good." Both camps support having the government manage, control, and prop up industry and commerce. In rhetoric, a vicious divide separates the two camps. Yet when in power, the two camps act much the same.

We need to know about libertarianism because it challenges ideas we take for granted. For instance, most assume that if some goal—such as national prosperity or helping the poor—is important, then the government should take charge of achieving that goal. In contrast, libertarians say that because these goals are so important, we must not let government take charge. When most Americans see a problem, they wonder how government could fix it. When libertarians see a problem, they wonder how it could be fixed.

We need to know about libertarianism because it challenges the status quo. We tend to take the status quo for granted. We see a world divided into powerful states, states that try to control and regulate many aspects of citizens' lives. We assume this is only natural and there are no alternatives. Libertarianism says we can and must do better.

We need to know about libertarianism because it challenges the authority of the rich and powerful. Most of us have a pro-authority bias. We evolved to conform to social pressure. Psychologist Stanley Milgram showed that most ordinary people are willing to torture and kill one another if a scientist tells them to. Despite the American creed of resisting government, Americans tend to defer to power. Libertarian ideas fight back against this bias.

We need to know about libertarianism to help determine whether our own moral and political beliefs are consistent. Libertarianism's basic ideas come from commonsense morality, yet libertarians use these ideas in ways that defy common sense. For example, commonsense morality says that if a person is minding his own business and isn't hurting anyone, he should be left alone. Yet most of us would imprison that person if we found out that, while minding his business and not hurting anyone, he also snorted some cocaine. As you'll see in reading this book, libertarians ground their arguments in premises and ideas you probably agree with. If so, you'll want to ask yourself why you are not a libertarian. Are the libertarians mistaken, or are you? (Or, on some issues are libertarians right, while on other issues they're not?)

We need to know more about libertarianism because most of us have mistaken ideas about what libertarians believe and why. Thirty years ago, hardly anyone discussed libertarian ideas in the mainstream press. Yet, in recent years, the press has had serious interest in libertarian thought. However, the press often fails to present libertarians in a fair way. Thus, there is a good chance that you misunderstand what libertarians actually think. *Slate*, the *Huffington Post*, the *New Yorker*, and the *Boston Review* published articles on libertarianism by libertarianism's critics. Libertarians believe these articles are as fair and balanced as the latest gossip column about Brad and Angelina's marital spats. Critics have weak incentives to characterize libertarianism fairly. Even if we reject libertarianism, we should know what we're rejecting.

We need to know about libertarianism because it—or parts of it—might be right.

5. Are there different kinds of libertarians?

Libertarians do not all agree on everything. "Libertarianism" is an umbrella term for a set of related political philosophies.

Libertarians divide into three main categories: (1) classical liberals, (2) hard libertarians, and (3) neoclassical liberals. The boundaries between these groups are fluid. They are set apart by their place in the history of libertarian thought. Each group also shares a set of core ideas.

1. *Classical liberals:* Classical liberals were the first libertarians. Classical liberal thinkers include Adam Smith, David Hume, John Locke, Mary Wollstonecraft, Harriet Taylor Mill, Frédéric Bastiat, and David Ricardo from the nineteenth century, as well as F. A. Hayek, James Buchanan, Gordon Tullock, and Milton Friedman from the twentieth century.

Classical liberals advocate open, tolerant societies; strong civil rights; strong economic and property rights; and open-market economies. They oppose war, imperialism, and conquest. They oppose government control and management of the economy. They oppose corporate welfare and crony capitalism.

Classical liberals are less opposed than hard libertarians to using government to solve problems. Nobel laureate economist Milton Friedman says, "...government may enable us at times to accomplish jointly what we would find difficult or expensive to accomplish severally. However, any such use of government is fraught with danger. We should not and cannot avoid using government in this way. But there should be a clear and large balance of advantages before we do." Classical liberals often believe the government should provide public goods (such as roads or national defense), a social safety net of some sort, and certain services, such as public schooling or, better yet, public vouchers for private schools. Classical liberals often accept some government regulation of the economy.

Classical liberals tend to argue that we should respect liberty because doing so tends to produce good consequences. They believe freedom is the soil in which virtue, culture, scientific progress, and prosperity best grow.

Note that the early classical liberals did not call themselves "classical liberals"—they just called themselves "liberals." The word "liberal" once meant what we now mean by "classical liberal." However, in the late nineteenth century, American social democrats co-opted the word "liberal" for themselves. The word "libertarian" developed in part because classical liberals needed to distinguish themselves from social democrats. To the typical American, "liberal" connotes someone who advocates an extensive welfare state, extensive government social services, strongly redistributive taxation, and strong government presence and management of the market economy. Classical liberals oppose each of these things.

2. *Hard libertarians:* In the middle of the twentieth century, one strain of classical liberalism developed into (what I will call) *hard libertarianism.* Hard libertarianism is a more radical version of classical liberal thought.

While classical liberals believe that property rights are important, they still believe that people could be taxed to provide for some minimal amount of public goods, welfare programs, and social services. In contrast, hard libertarians believe that all such taxes are morally equivalent to theft. For instance, imagine OxFam representatives came to your house, pointed a gun at you, and demanded you give their charity money. Even though you have a moral duty to help the poor, OxFam has no right to force you to help. The OxFam representatives are thieves, and they violate your rights. Hard libertarians say nothing changes if a government tax collector points the gun instead.

Hard libertarians thus tend to think the role for government is minimal. Many of them believe governments should provide only a court system, military protection, and police. These libertarians are said to advocate a "minimal" or "night watchman" state.

Some hard libertarians are anarchists. They believe society would function better and be more just if we dispensed with government. (See question 33.) A government is an institution that (1) claims a monopoly on the use of force, (2) claims a monopoly right to make rules and to issue commands to others, (3) expects others to comply with these rules and commands, and (4) has sufficient power to maintain these monopolies. Anarchist libertarians say that if private monopolies in business are bad, political monopolies on the use of coercive authority are even worse.

Compared to classical liberals, hard libertarians tend to ground their beliefs much more on a concern for people's rights and much less on a concern for producing good consequences. Still, hard libertarians also believe that a libertarian society would produce good consequences, better than any of the alternatives.

Hard libertarians include the novelist Ayn Rand, the economist Murray Rothbard, and the philosophers Robert Nozick and Eric Mack.

When you think of libertarianism, there's a good chance you think of what I call "hard libertarianism." However, hard libertarianism does not represent the mainline of broadly libertarian thinking. In some respects, it is an aberration inside classical liberal political thought.

3. *Neoclassical liberals:* A new form of classical liberal (i.e., libertarian) thinking emerged in the past 30 years. Many of these new classical liberals just call themselves classical liberals or libertarians. Some call themselves neoclassical liberals or bleeding-heart libertarians.

Neoclassical liberals share many of the same concerns of the classical liberals. However, what separates them from the older classical liberals is that they have an explicit, foundational concern for *social justice*. (See questions 75–77.)

At root, advocates of social justice believe that just social institutions must work sufficiently to the benefit of all, including the least advantaged and most vulnerable members of society. To believe in social justice is to hold that the distribution of benefits and burdens in society matters as a matter of justice. Like other libertarians, neoclassical liberals say that people are owed property rights as a matter of respect. However, they say, if a regime of private property systematically tended to leave large numbers of people destitute through no fault of their own, that regime would be illegitimate.

The idea of social justice is often associated with thinkers on the left, such as Marxists, left-liberals, or social democrats. Neoclassical liberals agree with Marxists, left-liberals, and social democrats that a just society must have institutions that sufficiently benefit the poor. However, neoclassical liberals think a concern for social justice not only is compatible with but also *requires* a commitment to open and free markets, strong property rights, and economic freedom.

Marxists say that if we want to realize social justice, we cannot have open markets and strong economic rights. Social democrats say that if we want to realize social justice, we must have highly managed and regulated markets and weaker economic rights. Yet, neoclassical liberals say that if we care about the poor and want to realize social justice, we *must* have open markets and strong economic rights. Neoclassical liberals say that if we care about the poor, the last thing we'd want to do is inflict Marxism upon them. The poor have flourished in commercial societies, and almost nowhere else.

We can distinguish among the three kinds of libertarians by their attitudes toward social justice. Neoclassical liberals explicitly *affirm* ideals of social justice. Hard libertarians explicitly *reject* ideals of social justice. (See questions 75–77.) Classical liberals are ambiguous about social justice. Many classical liberals wrote before the concept of social justice had developed. Classical liberals did not reject social justice so much as fail to consider it. However, most classical liberals are explicitly concerned about the poor. Adam Smith changed economics forever when he argued that the wealth of nations is measured not by the size of the king's treasury but by the fullness of the common man's stomach and by the opportunities available for his children. Classical liberals advocate classical liberal institutions in large part because they believe these institutions help the poor.

In popular discussions, people sometimes use "libertarian" in a narrow way, just to refer to hard libertarians. They sometimes use "libertarian" in a broader way, to refer to anyone who advocates free markets, property rights, and an open and tolerant society. This books uses "libertarian" in the broader sense, to include classical liberals, hard libertarians, and neoclassical liberals. At times, I will refer specifically to one of these three camps. When I describe what libertarians think, I generalize among them.

6. Are libertarians conservatives?

No. Libertarianism is not a right-wing or conservative view. Libertarians and certain conservatives share some political beliefs, but they are opposed on many others.

American conservatives often claim to be skeptical of government power. They worry that when government tries to solve problems, it often makes things worse rather than better. Conservatives often claim to favor free markets, less extensive government management and regulation of the economy, and strong respect for property rights. On these matters, libertarians and conservatives agree.

Yet, for many conservatives, talk about limited government is just talk. When in power, many conservatives violate these supposed commitments. They rig regulations and tax codes in ways that favor large, rich corporations over small businesses. They fund pork barrel projects and corporate welfare. They try to restrict foreign trade in order to help domestic producers. They restrict immigration, impose trade barriers and tariffs, and support economic subsidies to domestic companies. They seize private property for public works projects. Libertarians and conservatives both talk free-market talk, but libertarians mean it.

Conservatives also favor having a powerful police state and forceful, hawkish foreign policy. They want to be tough on crime, and in particular, tough on drugs. They want the United States to be a superpower that controls world affairs. They support initiating wars against other countries in order to maintain American dominance.

Libertarians say this undermines conservatives' claim that they are for small government. The War on Terror and War on Drugs lead to big government. Libertarians say that in practice, despite their rhetoric, conservatives tend to make government bigger and more obtrusive, not leaner and less obtrusive.

Many conservatives believe that the government should support and impose traditional Judeo-Christian values. Conservatives believe one of the main purposes of government is to reinforce citizens' moral virtue. For example, ultra-conservative presidential hopeful Rick Santorum says that US law must "comport with higher law" and that, if elected president, he would decide policy on the basis of "biblical truths." These culturally oriented conservatives tend to support school-sponsored prayer, oppose same-sex marriage, want to prevent homosexuals from holding government jobs or working in the military, want schools to teach creationism instead of science, and want to restrict the right to divorce. They favor forbidding sex work and want to regulate or forbid access to sexual materials.

Conservatives tend to support the Patriot Act, warrantless wiretapping, torture, Guantanamo Bay, and other violations of civil liberty in order to fight the War on Terror. They advocate a punitive police state and restricting defendants' ability to defend themselves. They advocate empowering the state to execute criminals. (Republican candidate Newt Gingrich once advocated executing all drug dealers.) They show little concern that their police state disproportionately burdens poor minorities. They seem unconcerned that despite having only about 5% of the world's population, the United States houses over half the world's prisoners. They reject women's rights, such as abortion rights or the right to access to contraception. They regard the American Civil Liberties Union with disgust.

For all these reasons, conservatives and libertarians are ideological foes.

Libertarians, unlike conservatives, advocate an expansive sphere of civil liberties. (See questions 44–61.)

Libertarians often do agree with some conservative beliefs. For instance, conservatives argue strong family ties, marriage, and stable homes are the bedrock of society. These ideas are not unique to conservatives, though. Most sociologists are on the left, yet, like conservatives, they argue (and have ample data showing) that unstable or broken homes cause crime, violence, poverty, and delinquency. Sociologists argue that children born to unmarried mothers have far worse life prospects than children born to married mothers. At least in the United States, men who do not work are less happy than men who work hard. Religious citizens report greater life satisfaction than secular citizens. All of these are stereotypically conservative claims, yet left-wing sociologists also tend to endorse them. Many libertarians do as well.

Still, libertarians, unlike conservatives, believe having government promote Judeo-Christian values will not solve social ills. Conservatives worry about broken homes. Libertarians believe conservative government is often the thing breaking the broken homes. For instance, libertarians believe the War on Drugs destroys and immiserates inner cities. (See question 50.) Also, libertarians, unlike conservatives, do not believe that a home with two mothers or two fathers is any more broken than a home with one mother and one father.

Conservatives want government to promote traditional virtues. Libertarians deny governments can do so in any direct way. For instance, suppose some people are genuinely lazy and choose not to work. A government could of course force them to work. But that would not make those people industrious or responsible. If you act responsibly only under threat of law, you are not actually responsible.

Many self-described conservatives will find my description of conservatism unfair. Some self-described conservatives oppose the Patriot Act, the union of religion and the state, civil rights abuses, and hawkish American foreign policy. They have no problem with the state recognizing same-sex marriage, as long as the state doesn't require churches to recognize such marriages. They might say that even though they believe abortion, prostitution, or gambling are morally wrong, they would not make these things illegal. However, a person who thinks this way is best described not as a political conservative, but as a political libertarian with morally conservative views.

7. Are libertarians liberals?

Yes and no—it depends on what we mean by "liberal."

In popular American politics, most people use "liberal" to describe anyone left of center, short of Marxists and communists. "Liberal" in this sense means a left-leaning person who advocates increased government control of the economy, an extensive welfare state, and a strong commitment to civil rights. Libertarians have an even stronger commitment to civil rights than left-liberals do, but they do not advocate government control of the economy or an extensive welfare state. So, they cannot be called "liberals" in this sense.

However, the word "liberal" has distinct meaning in political *philosophy*. When philosophers talk about liberalism, they do not mean what Rush Limbaugh or Jon Stewart mean. In the philosophical sense of "liberal," a liberal is a person who advocates liberty. Liberals regard liberty as the fundamental value by which to guide politics. They regard respect for liberty as the primary constraint on political action. A person is liberal to the extent she is committed to respecting and promoting personal freedom. In this sense, yes, all libertarians are liberals.

In philosophical liberalism, there is a divide between "left-liberals" and libertarians. This divide is over the issue of economic liberty.

Most liberals agree that some liberties are more important and more basic than others. These basic liberties merit a high degree of political protection. They can be infringed only in exceptional cases. On their lists of basic liberties, most liberals include not only some civil and political liberties but also some economic liberties, such as the right to own property.

Yet liberals differ about the *scope* of the basic economic liberties. Libertarians believe that our economic liberties should have a wide scope. Just as freedom of religion requires that people be given wide latitude to make religious decisions for themselves—without having to answer to or justify themselves to anyone—libertarians say that economic freedom requires that people be given wide latitude to make economic and financial decisions for themselves. Left-liberals believe our economic liberties should have a narrow scope. For example, the prominent left-liberal philosopher John Rawls argues that each person has a right to own personal property (such as toothbrushes or books) and to decide her own occupation. However, all other economic decisions belong not to private individuals, but to the government, or to all eligible voters, as a whole. For Rawls, the government gets to decide whether you may own a bakery or not.

Libertarians thus claim that, as a matter of basic justice, people have the right to acquire, hold, use, give, and in many cases destroy personal property; to acquire wealth for themselves; to make and enter into contracts; to buy and sell goods and services on terms to which all parties consent; to choose their occupation; to negotiate the terms under which they work; to manage their households as they see fit; to create things for sale; to start, run, and stop businesses; to own factories and businesses; to develop property for productive purposes; to take risks with capital; to speculate on commodities futures; to decide what to eat, drink, and wear; to determine what kinds of entertainment and cultural experiences they will consume; and more.

In contrast, left-liberals believe that as a matter of basic justice, people should only have the right to choose their own occupation and the right to own personal, nonproductive property. This does not mean that all or even most left-liberals are socialists. In fact, most left-liberals now advocate a market-based economy with private ownership of the means of production. Most left-liberals believe a market economy is necessary. They think there are no feasible alternatives. However, left-liberals advocate economic liberty in the market only to the extent that it helps the poor. They advocate market economies only to the extent this economic system promotes other goals of social justice. They do not think that such economic liberties are important as a way of showing respect for individual citizens. Libertarians typically agree that a market economy should help the poor, but they also believe that people have a basic right to make trades with others.

Many left-liberals believe that under a libertarian free market, large corporations would become too powerful and would seize control of politics. Like left-liberals, libertarians also worry that corporations can be too powerful and exert too much control on politics. Left-liberals propose to solve the problem by expanding the power of government to control corporations. Libertarians think this strategy backfires. They tend to think corporations will seize this very power in order to disadvantage their competitors and increase their own power. Libertarians believe that the Left's attempts to constrain corporate power actually increase corporate power. Libertarians also worry that that the left-liberal opposition to corporatism is disingenuous. Left-liberals often have power. When in power, they subsidize and bail out their favored corporations.

8. Is libertarianism a radical view?

The word "radical" has a few distinct meanings. Sometimes people use "radical" as a synonym for "Marxist." Libertarians are not Marxists—they believe Marxism violates people's rights and undermines social justice. So, they are not radical in that sense. But sometimes, by "radical," we mean a person who advocates drastic reforms. In that sense, yes, most libertarians are radicals.

Classical and neoclassical liberals are more moderate than hard libertarians, but libertarianism is not a moderate or centrist view. Libertarians advocate radical freedom, radical peace, radical respect, radical equality, and radical tolerance. Libertarians say there is nothing inherently good about being moderate on political issues. After all, the moderate position on, say, black civil rights is *Jim Crow*. The moderate position on free speech involves having an active board of government censors. The interventionist foreign policy of the United States over the past few decades is the moderate position between pacifism and imperialism.

Libertarianism is not a commonsense view, and yet its basic ideas are grounded in commonsense, day-to-day morality. As the libertarian economist Bryan Caplan says, consider what commonsense morality says about how we should treat strangers. We may not enslave them, steal from them, rape them, or attack them. We may not demand that they serve us. We may not force them to feed us or provide us with medical care. We may not punch them for holding different religious views than our own. We may not swat cigarettes or Big Macs out of their mouths, even if we are sure that cigarettes and Big Macs are bad for them. We may not chase them out of Best Buy for trying to buy imported stereos, nor may we stop them from taking jobs they want to take. We may not kidnap and force them to fight our enemies. We may not walk into their businesses and tell them how to run things.

All of these ideas are taken for granted in commonsense moral thinking. What makes libertarians radical is that they think these ideas also apply to the government and its agents. Suppose Alf doesn't want Betty to smoke cigarettes. Commonsense moral thinking holds that Alf is not allowed to push a gun in Betty's face to tell her she can't smoke. Now, suppose everyone except Betty votes to create the ATF, votes to give Alf an ATF uniform, and votes to have Alf take away Betty's cigarettes. Libertarians say nothing changes. Alf still may not stop Betty from smoking. We the people have commanded Betty to stop smoking, but, libertarians say, we have no right to issue this command, and Betty has no duty to obey. If anything, Betty should say to the rest of us, "How *dare* you? Who do you think you are?"

9. Are libertarians followers of Ayn Rand?

The novelist Ayn Rand (1905–1982) may be the most famous (or infamous) libertarian. Two of her novels, *The Fountainhead* and *Atlas Shrugged*, sell hundreds of thousands of copies per year. After 1957, Rand stopped writing novels and began writing nonfiction work on what she regarded as the philosophical themes expressed in her novels. (Some of her critics believe her explicit philosophy does not do justice to the ideas contained within the novels.) Rand's influence is enormous. For instance, US congresspersons Ron Paul and Paul Ryan and Supreme Court Justice Clarence Thomas claim her as among their main intellectual inspirations.

Rand rejected the label "libertarian" and did not want to be associated with libertarianism. She regarded most self-described libertarians as "whim-worshipping subjectivist[s]" and "monstrous, disgusting…people" who lacked proper philosophical foundations for their views. (In general, Rand was hostile to anyone who disagreed with her about anything.)

Despite her hostility to non-Objectivist libertarians, Rand is probably responsible for introducing more people, especially adolescents, to libertarian ideas than any other person. They find appealing ideas in Rand, such as the following:

- Individuals need to take responsibility for their own lives; they must not live as parasites off of others' efforts.
- It is wrong to initiate force against others.
- Productivity and creativity are important *moral* virtues.
- Integrity—remaining true to oneself—is a necessary part of the good life.
- Each of us has a right to pursue happiness. We are not born to serve others.

Many also agree with Rand's *moral* condemnation of socialism. For Rand, the problem with socialism is not just that it is inefficient. Rather, she regarded socialism as glorifying self-sacrifice.

Though she is influential, Rand does not represent the mainline of libertarian or more broadly classical liberal thinking. Rand was a "hard libertarian," and hard libertarianism is not the mainline of libertarian thinking. (See question 5.) In her later years, Rand styled herself as a philosopher, but most philosophers, including most libertarian philosophers, regard her philosophical work as poor.

Rand called her philosophy Objectivism. Objectivism's main ideas are that reality exists independently of any mind or anyone's beliefs about the world, that objective knowledge of the world is possible, that the individual people have a moral obligation to pursue their enlightened self-interest, and that only a laissez-faire capitalist political and economic regime is compatible with man's objective nature.

Most libertarians—and, indeed, most philosophers—accept that there is an objective reality about which we can have knowledge. Aside from Objectivists, few libertarians or others agree with Rand that our one and only moral obligation is to pursue our self-interest. (See question 25.) Libertarians generally agree with some, if not all, of Rand's conclusions about politics, but they often have different reasons for accepting those conclusions.

10. Is libertarianism a new view?

Classical liberalism—the earliest strand of libertarianism—developed in Europe in the late seventeenth century. Many founders of the United States were classical liberals.

Classical liberalism developed in part as a reaction to religious war. Between 1562 and 1598, millions died in the French Wars of Religion between Huguenots and Catholics. During the Thirty Years War—which began as a religious war—the population of what is now Germany dropped from about 21 million to 13.5 million. Nearly a third of the German towns and villages were destroyed. By the end of the century, people were exhausted from the bloodshed.

They realized that using war to save people's souls saved no one but damned many. As a result, many people began to believe that societies should tolerate diverse points of view and ways of living.

Under European feudalism, every person was bound by an oath to those above him. Monarchs justified their power as the will of God. Thinkers such as Thomas Hobbes and John Locke helped to undo these traditional ideas about the relationship of the individual to government. Hobbes and Locke argued that government has to justify itself to those governed on terms the governed could accept. They argued that rights are not mere legal conventions. Instead, each person had rights as a matter of justice.

The Scottish Enlightenment of the eighteenth century gave rise to Adam Smith (a moral philosopher who helped to found economics as a discipline), Adam Ferguson (a founder of sociology), and David Hume (a prominent historian and philosopher). These figures developed the idea that society is largely a *spontaneous order*. Society is not a machine designed by an engineer. It is more like an ecosystem. The languages we speak, the cultures we enjoy, and the shape of the economy as a whole are a product of human *action*, but not of human *design*. Just as park rangers cannot really manage a jungle ecosystem, so government bureaucrats cannot really manage an economy, a language, or a society.

Smith, Hume, and others in the Scottish Enlightenment wanted to know why some nations were rich and others poor. They believed that freedom explained the difference. An open market turns human energy and ingenuity away from destructive war and toward peaceful, mutually advantageous cooperation. Adam Smith's *Wealth of Nations* was revolutionary in part because Smith insisted we measure the wealth of nations not by the size of the king's palace but by the wealth and opportunity available to the king's subjects. *The Wealth of Nations* was also remarkable for its sustained critique of empire building and war.

11. What are some common criticisms of libertarianism?

Some critics claim libertarians have a single-minded obsession with liberty to the exclusion of other values. Most people agree that liberty matters, but it is not the only thing that matters.

Many critics believe that in a libertarian society, many of the poor would starve or at least be left destitute. They believe that extensive government management of the economy and a welfare state are necessary to save the poor. For example, the leftist philosopher Brian Barry accused the libertarian philosopher Robert Nozick of "...proposing to starve or humiliate ten percent or so of his fellow citizens (if he recognizes the word) by eliminating all transfer payments through the state, leaving the sick, the old, the disabled, the mothers with young children and no breadwinner, and so on, to the tender mercies of private charity, given at the whim and pleasure of the donors and on any terms that they choose to impose."

Left-liberals, Marxists, and social democrats regard libertarianism as only serving the rich and advantaged. Libertarianism serves big business and large corporations, but not the interests of the common person. They believe a libertarian regime would cause massive income inequality.

Many critics believe that libertarians are unusually selfish people. They think libertarians are opposed to helping others. They regard libertarianism as a defense of selfishness.

Conservative critics believe libertarianism would break down the social fabric. They think libertarianism would lead to widespread sexual promiscuity, sexual perversion, licentiousness, sacrilege, and drug use. They believe a libertarian culture would destroy traditional values.

Many conservatives and even many left-liberals oppose libertarianism because they regard it as too dovish on foreign policy. Under libertarian politics, the United States would not try to police the world or control world politics. It would deal with other nations only through trade. It would fight wars only in genuine self-defense, and only when there is a clear and imminent threat. Some conservatives thus worry libertarianism would allow China or Russia to dominate the world.

Many conservatives dislike libertarian views on immigration. Libertarians would allow free and open immigration. Conservatives believe this would cause high crime and would destroy the nation's culture. Many left-liberals and conservatives believe free immigration would make domestic wages plummet.

Overall, people on the left oppose libertarianism because they think it would cause inequality and would hurt the poor. People on the right oppose libertarianism because they think it would lead to moral depravity and a weak America.

12. What percentage of Americans are libertarians?

Researchers at the University of Michigan, Stanford University, and elsewhere conduct the American National Election Studies, an important survey of voter opinion. The surveys ask questions such as whether we should have more or less government control of the economy and whether we should be more or less tolerant of others.

Using this data, analysts at the CATO Institute, a libertarian (at least at the time I am writing this) think tank in Washington, DC, estimate that approximately 15% of voters qualify as libertarian. However, some other polls and surveys estimate that a larger percentage of voters are libertarian or libertarian leaning. Gallup polls generally identify 20–23% of voters as libertarian. A *Washington Post*-ABC News Poll conducted in 2007 found that roughly 26% of Americans are libertarian. (For more on this point, see question 94.)

Note that most people who have libertarian beliefs do not call themselves libertarian. They often call themselves liberals, conservatives, or moderates.

13. Who are some famous libertarians?

There are libertarians all over.

Few successful politicians are fully libertarian. The American political system tends to select for politicians who hold views that are relatively moderate and centrist (as measured against the voters in their districts). However, there are some libertarian-leaning politicians, including Gary Johnson, recent former governor of New Mexico; Craig Benson, recent former governor of New Hampshire; and US Representative Ron Paul. Representative Paul Ryan says Ayn Rand was one of his biggest influences.

The Left often regards libertarianism as serving the interests of big business. Still, most businesspeople in the United States are run-of-the-mill Democrats or Republicans. Some libertarian business leaders include John Allison (of BB&T), John Mackey (of Whole Foods), and Peter Thiele (of PayPal).

There are many libertarians in popular culture. Libertarian novelists and writers include Ayn Rand, Dean Koontz, Robert Heinlein, Dave Barry, and P. J. O'Rourke. Libertarian television, film, and radio stars include Penn Jillette and Teller, Chris Rock, Clint Eastwood, Drew Carey, Kurt Russell, Tommy Chong, Trey Parker and Matt Stone (creators and voices of *South Park*), John Stossel, and Howard Stern.

Libertarian musicians include Neil Peart (of Rush), Dwight Yoakam, and John Popper (of Blues Traveler).

There are also a large number of libertarian academics, including the economists Gary Becker, Tyler Cowen, and Steven Landsburg; philosophers David Schmidtz, Gerald Gaus, Loren Lomasky, and Michael Huemer; sociologists Charles Murray and Fabio Rojas; political scientists Michael Munger and Mark Pennington; and legal theorists Richard Epstein, Randy Barnett, John Hasnas, and Ilya Somin.

2

THE NATURE AND
VALUE OF LIBERTY

14. How do libertarians define "liberty"?

Philosophers say there are two major kinds of liberty: negative liberty and positive liberty.

We often use the words "liberty" or "freedom" to refer to an absence of obstacles, impediments, or constraints. Philosophers call this *negative liberty*. So, for instance, a person enjoys freedom of speech—understood as a negative liberty—when others do not stop her from speaking her mind. Free speech is the absence of interference with one's speech.

In contrast, *positive liberty* is the power or capacity to do as one chooses. For instance, when we talk about being "free as a bird," we mean that the bird has the *power* or ability to fly. We do not mean to say that people rarely interfere with birds.

Negative liberty is the *absence* of obstacles; positive liberty is the *presence* of powers or abilities.

A person has freedom of property—understood as a positive liberty—if she actually owns and controls some property. John Kerry and the average Democratic voter both have the negative liberty to own yachts—no one would try to stop them from buying one—but only Kerry can actually afford a yacht. He thus has the power to do something most of his constituents cannot, and in that respect he has more positive liberty than they do.

Until recently, most libertarians tended to argue that the only real kind of liberty is negative liberty. They believed the concept of positive liberty was confused. For a long time, the status quo was that libertarians and classical liberals advocated a negative conception of liberty, while left-liberals, socialists, and Marxists advocated a positive conception of liberty.

Recently, though, many libertarians have begun to accept *both* negative and positive liberty. When contemporary libertarians say they want a free society, they mean that they want both (1) a society in which people do not interfere with each other and (2) a society in which most people have the means and ability to achieve their goals.

15. Why do some libertarians reject positive liberty?

Until recently, most libertarians rejected the concept of positive liberty. They said positive liberty was not a genuine form of liberty. They agreed that the power to achieve one's ends was important. They agreed that personal autonomy was important. However, they thought that if positive liberty—understood as the power to achieve one's ends—counted as a form of liberty, this would automatically license socialism and a heavy welfare state. Since they opposed socialism and a heavy welfare state, they rejected the concept of positive liberty.

Marxists and other socialists argue that a commitment to positive liberty implies a commitment to socialism. Their argument is simple:

1. Government ought to guarantee everyone has full liberty.
2. One form of liberty is positive liberty.
3. Therefore, government ought to guarantee everyone has positive liberty.

4. In order for government to guarantee that everyone has positive liberty, it must manage the economy and provide extensive welfare benefits.

5. Therefore, government must manage the economy and provide extensive welfare benefits.

This argument is valid. That is, the conclusion follows from the premises. Thus, if libertarians want to reject the conclusion, they must reject at least one of the premises. In the past, libertarians tended to reject premise 2. They insisted that positive liberty was not really a form of liberty at all.

16. Why do many libertarians now accept positive liberty?

Question 14 explains the distinction between negative and positive liberty. Question 15 explains why many libertarians used to reject positive liberty.

Contemporary libertarian thinkers tend to embrace positive liberty. They agree that the power to achieve one's goals really is a form of liberty. They agree with Marxists and socialists that this form of liberty is valuable, and that negative liberty without positive liberty is often of little value.

However, contemporary libertarians say, the claim that positive liberty is valuable implies *nothing* about what the government should or should not do. We cannot determine what government should do about liberty just by settling on a definition of the word "liberty." To know what government should do, if anything, about a particular kind of liberty, we must instead examine historical, sociological, and economic evidence to see what actually happens when people rely on government to play a given role. It may then turn out that government should do *nothing* to promote positive liberty. Or it may turn out that government should promote positive liberty *indirectly*.

Do we want government to issue a legal guarantee that we all will have significant positive liberty? In a recent book, philosopher David Schmidtz and I argue that the answer depends on what happens when government issues legal guarantees. A legal guarantee is just a legal declaration. It is no real guarantee. (Consider that the Soviet Constitution of 1936 "guaranteed" free speech, privacy, and due process.) Many factors can and do disrupt, corrupt, or pervert legal guarantees. Legal guarantees are good only if they work. To give government the power to promote some valuable end does not automatically promote that end. In fact, sometimes, giving government the power to promote an end undermines that end.

Schmidtz and I argue that, as a matter of historical fact, protecting negative liberties is the most important and effective way of promoting positive liberty. The way governments best promote positive liberty is to uphold the rule of law, property rights, freedom, tolerance, and open markets. In contrast, Schmidtz and I say, socialist societies have never helped their citizens enjoy much positive liberty. Thus, a commitment to positive liberty does not *license* socialism; it *forbids* it. Marxists say that positive liberty is the only real liberty. Schmidtz and I counter that this real liberty is found in market societies, and almost nowhere else.

Sophisticated nonlibertarians respond that of course legal guarantees are no real guarantees, and of course protecting negative liberty is essential to promoting positive liberty. However, they argue, that as an empirical matter, we need extensive government intervention and a strong welfare state to make sure everyone benefits from a market economy and from their negative liberty.

17. Why do libertarians think liberty is so important?

Libertarians value liberty for two different kinds of reasons:

1. *Freedom shows respect:* Libertarians say that in order to respect others as members of the moral community and

as ends in themselves, we owe them an extensive sphere
of personal liberty.
2. *Freedom produces good consequences:* Libertarians say that
giving everyone a wide sphere of liberty produces better consequences than a more restricted sphere.

Hard libertarians tend to emphasize arguments that freedom is necessary to show respect for others. Classical
liberals tend to emphasize how freedom produces good
consequences.

1. First, let us consider how freedom might be necessary
as a matter of respect. Libertarians argue that each person
has an inviolability, founded on justice. We cannot force
some people to sacrifice themselves just so others may enjoy
greater welfare. We cannot treat individuals as tools to be
exploited and discarded so as to promote the good of others.
The rights secured by justice must not be subject to political
bargaining or to the calculus of social interests. We must not
subjugate others and force them to live by our will rather
than their own.

Each of us has our own life to lead. So long as we respect
others' rights, we must be permitted to live as we see fit. Most
libertarians agree that we have moral obligations to be charitable and to help others. However, they say, we cannot in general be forced to help others. Many people, when free, will
make self-destructive or heartless choices. However, libertarians say, to respect others as equals, we must allow others to
live as they choose, even if they choose vicious lives.

Libertarians advocate liberty in part as a response to the
problem of pervasive disagreement. People reasonably disagree about the nature of justice, the good life, and the good
community. Libertarians believe we must live together only on
terms all reasonable people can accept. Because we reasonably
disagree about the good and the just, coercion is only rarely
justified. To respect people as equal members of the moral

community, we must not subjugate them to our own wills. We must instead grant each person a large sphere of personal liberty.

Some critics of libertarianism claim that real freedom is not just about being left alone. Rather, freedom only matters if people have enough wealth and opportunity to enjoy their freedom. They think that in practice, libertarianism would prevent most people from enjoying this real freedom.

2. Second, consider consequentialist reasons for advocating liberty. Libertarians believe that granting everyone a wide scope of liberty generally produces good consequences. They believe that restrictions on liberty generally produce bad consequences. Libertarians argue that free societies produce greater wealth, happiness, prosperity, peace, good character, scientific knowledge, and generalized trust than unfree societies. For example, libertarians claim that societies with largely free-market economies (such as Switzerland, Canada, and Australia) have happier, healthier, and more prosperous citizens than societies with unfree economies (such as North Korea, Cuba, and Myanmar).

Libertarians admit that liberty does not always produce good results. Freedom does not always promote welfare. Permitting people to do as they please does not always make them better off. After all, if people are free, then they will often make stupid, imprudent, and self-destructive choices.

Yet, libertarians argue, allowing people to make stupid, imprudent, and self-destructive choices actually produces better results than trying to force people only to make smart, prudent, and safe choices. This is one reason libertarians want to end the War on Drugs. Libertarians agree that when people are allowed to use drugs, many of them will destroy their lives. But, libertarians argue, when the government forbids people from using drugs, even more lives are destroyed. (See question 50.)

Libertarians say that how much power government should have depends on what government will do with that power.

If power did not tend to corrupt (or attract the already corrupted), or if leaders were omniscient and unfailingly altruistic, we might want to entrust government with extensive power over our lives.

However, in the real world, power does corrupt and does attract the corrupted. In government, the power to do good is also the power do evil. This power will attract both those who want to do good and those who want to do evil. Would-be heroes and villains will thus compete for that power. Villains have an advantage when competing: They are willing to do whatever it takes, uninhibited by moral constraints.

In the real world, politicians, bureaucrats, and voters are often incompetent. Politicians are experts at winning elections, but not experts at running economies or managing health care. If the voting public were well informed and highly rational about politics, they would elect brilliant leaders. But, libertarians think (in light of social scientific studies), voters are largely ignorant and irrational. They thus choose bad leaders.

Libertarians are often accused of being overly optimistic about markets. Yet libertarians recognize that markets fail. Economics textbooks say that when markets fail, this can sometimes justify government intervention to correct the failure. However, these textbooks often just mean that, in principle, a well-informed and well-intentioned government could fix the problem. But real-world governments are not like textbook governments. Government leaders often do not know how to fix problems. When we give them the power to fix our problems, they often use that power for their own ends instead. Libertarians say that just as markets can and do fail, governments can and do fail. Libertarians believe that once we take into account both market and government failures, we should strongly favor free markets and rarely favor government intervention.

Some critics of libertarianism agree that governments can fail just as markets fail. But they disagree about the balance of the evidence. They think market failures tend to be more severe and government failures tend to be less severe. They thus advocate more government intervention and less free markets.

18. Do libertarians think liberty is the only value?

No. Most libertarians believe that liberty is just one value among many. Libertarians value liberty in part because they believe liberty produces *other* values. (See question 17.) Libertarians believe greater liberty generally leads to greater health, wealth, knowledge, innovation, and happiness.

19. Do libertarians believe liberty trumps all other values?

Economist Jeffrey Sachs complains that libertarians have a single-minded obsession with liberty. In contrast, Sachs believes we should often limit liberty to achieve other values. Sometimes liberty gets in the way of more important things. Sachs regards libertarians as saying, "Liberty at any cost! Liberty though the sky falls!" Sachs says that for libertarians, "compassion, justice, civic responsibility, honesty, decency, humility, and even survival of the poor, weak, and vulnerable—are all to take a back seat" to liberty.

Economist Steve Horwitz responds that we are not faced with the choice between a humane society or a free society. Instead, libertarians believe a free society is the *means* to achieving a humane society. Libertarians have an *empirical* disagreement with Sachs—they disagree about how the world works. Sachs thinks we must put some liberty aside in order to have compassion and justice and to help the poor. Libertarians believe that if we want to have compassion or justice or to help the poor, we need more liberty, not less.

Most libertarians agree that at least sometimes liberty should be sacrificed for other values. So, for instance, as the libertarian philosopher Dan Russell argues, in an emergency situation, sometimes property rights should be suspended. However, he says, if we ever want to escape such emergencies, or if we want to reduce the chances we will create emergencies, we need to create and respect property rights.

Libertarians add that conflict between liberty and other values is not a given. Instead, governments often *create* these conflicts. A policy of respecting liberty tends to minimize these conflicts.

For instance, consider the US War on Terror. Many claim that we must sacrifice some liberty to gain security. Libertarians say the US government created the conflict between liberty and security. In the past, it chose security over liberty and got neither. Libertarians say that the United States spent the past 50 years imposing embargoes upon, bullying, and murdering civilians in the Middle East. This induced Al Qaeda to attack and kill American civilians. (For instance, the United States imposed economic sanctions on Iraq after the first Iraq war. As political scientist John Mueller has documented, these sanctions caused hundreds of thousands of innocent Iraqi civilians to die. Osama bin Laden justified the 9/11 attacks in part as a response to these deadly sanctions.) The United States reacted to 9/11 by starting two wars. Perhaps this will make the US more secure. Many libertarians suspect it will instead breed the next generation of terrorists, who grow up wanting revenge after seeing their parents and siblings die from American bombs.

Or, consider US housing policy and the government's reaction to the 2008 financial crisis. Many claim we must now sacrifice some freedom in the market to ensure economic prosperity. Libertarians say the reason we are *now* asked to choose between liberty and prosperity is that in the *past*, we chose prosperity over liberty (and got neither). The government pushed for loose credit in the housing market. Before the financial crisis, libertarians argued that the 1995 modifications to the Community Reinvestment Act would push creditors to make overly risky loans. They said that the government-sponsored enterprises (GSEs) Freddie Mac and Fannie Mae would create moral hazard, because private investors knew they could issue risky loans and then sell those loans to the GSEs. Long before the housing market bubbled and burst, libertarians (such as Ron Paul and Peter Schiff) argued that government housing policies would cause a crisis. (See question 92.) At the time, they were seen as silly, uncaring alarmists. But they were right.

20. Do libertarians think our only moral duty is to respect others' liberty?

Most libertarians share commonsense moral concerns. They hold, like most others do, that we have duties to provide for charity, to avoid free-riding on others' efforts, to treat others with respect and kindness, to provide for our children and loved ones, and so on.

What makes libertarians distinct from other philosophical liberals, and especially from nonliberals, is that they think each human being has a very extensive sphere of personal liberty. Each person has strong rights against being interfered with, exploited, subjugated, or coerced. These rights cannot easily be overridden.

Rights act as side constraints on our actions. Rights forbid us from doing things to other people, even when doing these things would serve the common good or serve those other people's good.

So, for example, imagine I am a supremely expert life coach. Imagine that I can determine what is the happiest and best way for every person to live. Suppose I know with certainty that talented David would do much more good as a doctor than as a beach bum. Suppose I also know with certainty that David would be much happier and better off as a doctor than as a beach bum. However, suppose David wants to be a beach bum. Libertarians say that even under these circumstances, I may not force David to become a doctor. He has the right to choose, his own way of life, even though I know how to run his life better than he does.

To take another example, according to commonsense moral thinking, I may not steal food from your refrigerator in order to feed the homeless, even though the homeless value the food more than you do. Or, to take another example, even if it turned out that slavery or Jim Crow laws were economically efficient, this would not justify those institutions. Or, we may not force two people to get married, even if we somehow knew that they would be happiest together rather than apart.

Note that even if I believe it is wrong to force you to help the homeless, this does not imply I don't care about the homeless. In the same vein, if I am unwilling to force you to marry your "soul mate," that does not mean I am indifferent to your happiness. Rather, it means that there are limits on what I may force you to do, for your good or for the good of others.

21. What is the "presumption of liberty"?

Libertarianism is a *liberal* political philosophy. (See question 7.) All philosophical liberals believe that liberty is a fundamental value and that each person is endowed, as a matter of justice, with an extensive set of basic rights and liberties.

Liberals believe there is a strong presumption in favor of liberty. The presumption of liberty holds that, by default, people should be free to live as they see best, without having to ask permission from or justify themselves to other people. By default, *all* restrictions on liberty are presumed wrong and unjust until shown otherwise. The presumption of liberty holds that any restriction on liberty must be justifiable to those whose liberty is restricted. It holds that coercion—which nearly always limits freedom—must be justified. It follows that political authority and all laws are assumed unjustified until shown otherwise.

Liberals say, "For any activity X, by default, we should allow X. The onus is on society to justify a prohibition against X." In contrast, nonliberals say, "By default, we should forbid X until it's shown that allowing X serves some higher values or the common good." Liberal societies say, "We'll let you do X unless we can show that there is a conclusive moral reason—a reason you yourself must accept—against allowing you to do X." Nonliberal societies say, "We'll let you do X only if you give us good reasons to let you."

22. What rights do libertarians think we have?

Libertarians believe that, as a matter of justice, each person enjoys an extensive set of rights. These rights include the civil, economic, and political liberties.

The civil liberties include the right to free speech, right of free assembly, right of association, freedom of conscience, right of bodily integrity and freedom from abuse and assault, freedom of lifestyle choice, rights to protest, the right to exit (i.e., the right to leave a country and to renounce citizenship), and freedom of sexual choice. Libertarians also advocate liberal procedural rights in the criminal justice system, including rights against unwarranted search and seizure, the right to a fair and expeditious trial, the right to be presumed innocent until proven guilty, the right to hear and question one's accusers, and the right to habeas corpus. Libertarians generally oppose the death penalty and harsh criminal justice measures.

Libertarians advocate equal protection for homosexuals, and thus support same-sex marriage and oppose the US military's former restrictions on homosexuality. Libertarians advocate women's reproductive freedom, including the rights to have abortions, use birth control, and have sex on mutually acceptable terms. Libertarians oppose censorship, including Internet censorship, restrictions on pornography (provided the pornographic models are consenting adults), and restrictions on flag burning or government sedition.

Libertarians believe that people have the right to use drugs and make self-destructive choices. Libertarians oppose compulsory national service and the draft. Libertarians oppose the Patriot Act and government spying on Americans.

Libertarians also support free immigration. They believe people have a right to cross borders as they see fit. They hold a Mexican has the same right to live in the United States as a native-born American. They believe everyone has the right to take employment in any other country, regardless of citizenship. They hold that, except in special circumstances, governments may not forbid citizens from leaving a country, nor may governments forbid foreigners from entering. (See question 86.)

Libertarians interpret economic liberty as having the same wide scope as civil liberties. Just as all liberals agree that recognizing religious liberty requires the general protection of independent activity in the religious realm, libertarians claim that economic liberty requires the general protection of independent activity in economic matters.

Libertarians thus claim that, as a matter of basic justice, people have the right to acquire, hold, use, give, and in many cases destroy personal property; to acquire wealth for themselves; to make and enter into contracts; to buy and sell goods and services on terms to which all parties consent; to choose their occupation; to negotiate the terms under which they work; to manage their households as they see fit; to create things for sale; to start, run, and stop businesses; to own private property in the means of production; to develop property for productive purposes; to take risks with capital; to decide what to eat, drink, and wear; to determine what kinds of entertainment and cultural experiences one will consume; and more. (See question 62.) Libertarians believe that people have the right to sell sexual services or even their own body parts, such as kidneys. (See questions 51 and 52.)

Libertarians, like all liberals, believe there is a strong presumption in favor of liberty. Libertarians think that unless (1) an action coerces others or violates their rights or (2) there is a very strong independent justification for forbidding a certain action, then a person should be free to do that action.

Libertarians' attitudes toward political liberties—the right to vote and run for office—are mixed. Civil and economic liberties (as defined previously) give individuals power over themselves and create a sphere of personal autonomy that others must not violate. The political liberties—the rights to vote and to hold office if elected or selected—are different. They give individuals power over others. Thus, libertarians do not believe these liberties have the same kind of status as other liberties. Instead, many libertarians advocate democracy and the attendant political liberties for instrumental reasons—they think democracies better protect our rights than the alternatives. However, some libertarians are anarchists. (See question 33.) Some libertarians even believe that certain non-democratic governments could in principle be justified instead of democracy.

Most of the rights listed previously are *negative rights*. Negative rights forbid us from doing certain things to others. A person has a negative right to do or have something when others have *enforceable* duties not to interfere with her doing or having that thing. For example, your right to own your car forbids me from using it without your consent. Your right to life forbids me from killing you. Your right to sexual choice forbids me from deciding when and how you will have sex.

In contrast to negative rights are *positive rights*. A person has a positive right to something when others have *enforceable* duties to provide that thing to that person. For example, if you had a positive right to food, then it is permissible to force other people to give you food.

All libertarians believe we have positive rights against one another in special circumstances. For instance, libertarians believe parents have enforceable duties to care for their children. However, libertarians disagree about whether people have any general positive liberties held against society as a whole. Consider, for instance, the question of whether a destitute person can have the right to welfare payments from the state, or whether children have the right to be provided free education from the state. Hard libertarians generally deny that there are any such positive rights. In contrast, classical and neoclassical liberals do believe there are some such rights.

Note that when libertarians say each person has an extensive set of rights, they are talking about *moral* rights, what we owe to each other as a matter of justice and morality. They are not talking about the law or the Constitution. So, if you hear a libertarian say, "I have the right to smoke marijuana," she does not mean to say that the Constitution allows her to smoke marijuana. Similarly, if she says, "Jews in Nazi Germany had the right to life," she does not mean that concentration camps violated German law. She is making claims about justice, not claims about the law. Libertarianism is a political philosophy, not a theory of constitutional law.

23. Do libertarians believe rights are absolute?

To say a right is absolute is to say that it can never be outweighed by a competing consideration. That is, it is always wrong to violate the right, no matter what other moral considerations are at play. Thus, for example, if property rights are absolute, then it would be wrong to steal an ear of corn from a farmer to feed a starving child.

Some hard libertarians believe our rights, or at least many of our rights, are absolute. They believe it is always wrong to violate rights, no matter what.

However, libertarians generally believe rights are *not* absolute. Instead, they hold that our rights are (what philosophers call) *prima facie* rights. When a person has a prima facie right to do X, then there is a strong presumption in favor of allowing her to do X, but at least sometimes other moral considerations can override this presumption. For example, my right to property allows me to exclude other people from using my property. My property right in my lawn forbids you from walking on my lawn without my permission. However, suppose you were being chased by a mugger and needed to cross my lawn to get away. If my property rights were absolute, it would be wrong for you to run across my law as you flee. However, suppose my property rights are prima facie rights rather than absolute rights. Then, in order to flee the muggers, you could rightly cross the lawn, even without my permission, or even if I demanded you stay off the lawn.

Philosophers tend to think most moral obligations are prima facie rather than absolute. For instance, if you promise to meet me for dinner at 6 p.m., then by default, you should meet me at the promised time. You should not break your promise for just any old reason, such as that you decided you would rather eat with someone else. However, suppose you had a heart attack on the way to dinner. Or, suppose on the way to dinner, you come across a hurt child who needs help. In these cases, it seems permissible for you to break your promise. Other moral considerations outweigh your prima facie obligation to arrive on time.

3

HUMAN NATURE AND ETHICS

24. Do libertarians believe everyone is selfish?

A popular misconception holds that libertarians believe everyone is selfish all the time. According to this misconception, libertarians believe altruism is an illusion. Whenever a person seems to act for the sake of others, she in fact only intends her own good.

However, few libertarians endorse this view of human nature. Libertarians in general have no unusual views about human motivation. They are happy to defer to psychologists on this issue. Psychology tells us most people are predominantly selfish, but they also have altruistic motives, as well as motives that are neither selfish nor altruistic.

If this is a misconception, why is it so widespread?

First, libertarians often argue from economic theory. Economists often *model* human behavior *as if* people were always selfish. Economists know that people have a mix of motives. However, economic models that pretend everyone is selfish have strong predictive power. Because libertarians often use economic reasoning when defending their philosophy, they may appear to endorse the view that everyone is always selfish.

Second, libertarians are not romantic about politics. Libertarians believe that nothing magical happens to people's motivations when they enter politics. If people are predominantly selfish outside of politics, we should presume them to be predominantly selfish inside politics, at least until we have evidence otherwise. Libertarians thus often say that political institutions should *economize* on virtue. That is, when choosing among different kinds of institutions, we should not select institutions that require heavy doses of good will and altruism to succeed. If a political institution or policy requires heavy doses of good will and altruism to succeed, it won't succeed.

Nonlibertarians tend to imagine that because government is supposed to promote the common good, then politicians (or at least *their* favored politicians), government agents, police officers, voters, and soldiers must be unusually altruistic and public-spirited. Libertarians do not assume that soldiers or police officers are more saintly than the rest of us. Instead, they say political power attracts people who want to exploit that power for their own private ends.

25. Do libertarians believe everyone should be selfish?

Libertarians are not merely accused of believing everyone *is* selfish. (See question 24.) Another misconception holds that libertarians believe everyone *ought* to be selfish. Many people believe libertarians glorify selfishness.

That is a mistake. In general, libertarians have no unusual views about selfishness. Most libertarians think we have moral duties to promote others' welfare. Most libertarians believe we have strong duties of charity and duties to serve the common good. Most libertarians believe that only a monster or sociopath would lack concern for others.

Most libertarians agree that we owe some charity to others, but they disagree about just how much. However, this kind of disagreement isn't special to libertarians. Nonlibertarians also disagree. For instance, the philosopher

Peter Singer thinks we should never acquire luxury goods when we could instead use the money to save those in desperate need. Most other philosophers and other people, regardless of their political leanings, believe our duties of charity are much weaker.

Libertarianism in fact demands unselfish behavior. Libertarians denounce politicians who just want power for themselves. They denounce businesspeople who seek special favors from government in order to increase their profits. Libertarianism demands that everyone tolerate lifestyles they dislike.

Economics holds that when people pursue their self-interest through the free market, they also tend to promote the common good. Libertarians accept this point, and so are often less averse to self-interest than many on the left. The Left tends to see markets as zero-sum games where one person can make herself better off only by hurting others. The Left tends to think markets make winners only by making losers. Libertarians instead accept the idea from mainstream economics that the market is a positive sum game, where everyone can win all at once. However, none of this implies libertarians believe everyone should be selfish all the time.

Many people associate libertarianism with Ayn Rand. The hard libertarian novelist Ayn Rand advocated an unusual moral theory called *ethical egoism*. Ethical egoism claims that people should only pursue their enlightened, rational self-interest. Though Rand is an ethical egoist, and though many libertarians enjoy her novels, this does not mean all or even most libertarians are ethical egoists. Rand does not represent the mainline of libertarian or classical liberal thinking.

Rand argues that selfishness is a virtue. She believes every person has only one moral obligation: to promote his or her own self-interest. On its face, this theory of ethics is clearly false. If ethical egoism were true, then, if torturing babies would benefit me ever so slightly, I would be permitted to do so. However, it's clearly wrong for me to torture babies to get a slight benefit for myself, and so ethical egoism is false.

However, this objection may not be fair to Rand. Rand has an esoteric conception of self-interest. She does not seem to mean what most other people mean by "selfish." For instance, Rand seems to believe it is logically impossible for a person to benefit on net from taking or acquiring something he does not deserve. She thinks it is logically impossible for a person to benefit on net from aggressing against, abusing, or exploiting others. Rand thinks selfishness requires that we respect others' rights. She even believes that selfish people can authentically love one another, and that a truly selfish person would be willing to die to protect his or her loved ones. Whatever the merits or demerits of Rand's conception of selfishness, she does not regard sociopaths or predators as moral exemplars.

26. Are libertarians themselves unusually selfish?

Critics often say that libertarianism is just an attempt to rationalize greed and selfishness. For instance, the conservative Michael Gersen, a former speechwriter for George W. Bush, asserts that people turn to libertarianism during late adolescence because adolescents are egoistical and self-centered.

Libertarians are at base no different from anyone else. Some socialists are loving and kind people. Others are callous and cold-hearted. Some egalitarians help others. Others live haughty lifestyles and have disdain for the poor. Some conservatives are virtuous. Others are cruel.

In principle, social scientists could study whether people of some ideologies tend to be more selfish than others. As far as I know, no one has done so. So, if we ask whether libertarians are more selfish than others, the answer is that we do not know, and we do not have any reason to think they are.

We might try to study whether libertarians act more or less selfishly than others. For instance, we might examine whether they give more to charity than others. We know political conservatives give more money to charity (and are more likely to volunteer or donate blood) than those on the left. Less is known about how often and how much libertarians give.

Still, the conservative social scientist Arthur Brooks claims that, even once we control for income and other demographic factors, (1) supporters of free markets are much more likely to give to charity than those who oppose free markets, and (2) free marketers give greater amounts to charity than those who oppose free markets. All things equal, he says, supporters of the free market give more frequently and give larger amounts than others.

If Brooks is right, it's tempting to conclude free-market supporters are thus more selfless and benevolent than socialists and members of the Left. After all, donating to charity costs real wealth. If I give thousands to charity, that's a vacation I don't take. In contrast, to *advocate* or *vote for* a welfare state with high tax rates costs me nothing. Suppose a left-liberal votes for a candidate who promises to triple her taxes and give the proceeds to the poor. Her vote has almost zero chance of changing her actual tax rates. (The Left thus should be careful in accusing libertarians of selfishness.)

However, we should not rush to this conclusion. Perhaps the Left gives less because they believe private charity does not work. On their behalf, we might say: If you refuse to throw money at what you regard as bad medicine, this does not show you are indifferent to the disease.

Libertarians come across as selfish to the Left because (1) libertarians defend institutions the Left believes harm the poor, and (2) libertarians often criticize institutions the Left believes help the poor. For instance, libertarians often criticize the welfare state. To the Left, this comes across as callous indifference to the plight of the poor. Yet most libertarians criticize the welfare state because they believe the welfare state hurts the poor more than it helps them. If libertarians refuse to throw money at what they regard as bad medicine, this does not show they are indifferent to the disease.

The libertarian economist Milton Friedman, a Nobel laureate, wanted to replace most of the welfare state with a negative income tax. A negative income tax gives the poor who make less than a specified amount an unconditional cash grant to bring them up to that level. The poor are free to do as they please with the cash—including investing it and starting businesses. In contrast, the American welfare state provides a largely uniform package of benefits: food stamps, free health insurance, reduced housing costs, and the like. Friedman thought these programs might keep the poor from starving, but they do not lift the poor out of poverty, in part because they don't allow the poor to make entrepreneurial choices. These welfare programs respond to the emergency of dire poverty but never make the emergency go away. Friedman believed that the American welfare state trapped the poor in poverty.

Or, consider that most people think sweatshops are evil and should be shut down. In contrast, the philosopher Matt Zwolinski argues that if we try to shut down sweatshops, we will harm rather than help the world's most vulnerable workers. If we demand sweatshops have first-world labor standards, then these factories will not hire the poorest people, the people who most desperately need a job. Libertarians defend sweatshops out of concern for the poor. However, the anti-sweatshop movement suspects libertarians just want cheaper clothes.

When members of the Left want government to help people, they seek to have government do so in the most direct way: through handouts. Libertarians argue the best way to help the poor is indirect. Left-liberals say, "Let's help the poor by giving them health insurance." Libertarians say, "Let's help by creating background conditions that generate so much wealth that no one needs a handout." Left-liberals say, "Let's give the poor free food." Libertarians say, "Let's create background conditions that make the poor rich so they can buy their own food." To the Left, this comes across as special pleading for selfishness.

In political debates, all sides tend to be suspicious of the other sides' motives. Psychologists have shown that most of us are biased to believe that people who hold political views contrary to ours must be stupid, irrational, and evil. It is thus no surprise that members of the Left tend to think libertarians are selfish. They regard their own political beliefs as the only sensible expression of benevolence. They thus conclude libertarians must be selfish and cold-hearted.

Libertarians are also suspicious of the Left. Libertarians do not take it for granted that social democrats are benevolent or truly concerned for social justice. From the libertarian point of view, whenever the Left has power—and it frequently does—it seems all too eager to grant special favors to elite financiers, corporations, and special interests. Worse, many on the left oppose free immigration. To libertarians, this makes the Left's expression of concern for the poor seem disingenuous. Libertarians believe immigration restrictions remove the world's poorest people's chance for a better life. They believe immigration restrictions expose the world's poor to abuse and exploitation. (See question 86.) From the libertarian point of view, the Left seems to be obsessed with participatory democracy and nationalism. The Left seems to care more about making the relatively rich lower classes of the first world become slightly better off than with helping the truly poor of the third world.

Libertarians also are suspicious that the Left supports extensive welfare states just because the Left wants to *seem* benevolent. After all, if I publically advocate a welfare state, people will tend to assume I am a loving and kind person. I can feel good about myself, even if I haven't actually done anything to help anyone. It is cheap and easy for me to advocate having people fed. I get to enjoy the warm glow of benevolence at no cost to myself. On the other hand, if I actually donate money to help others, then I bear a real cost.

27. Why do some critics believe libertarians have an overly optimistic view of human nature?

Libertarians advocate a peaceful society with only a minimal amount of coercion. They are optimistic about human creativity and about unleashed people being able to solve their own problems.

Few libertarians think all problems would be solved overnight if only the world became libertarian. However, libertarians tend to trust voluntary cooperation far more than people on the left or right. Libertarians tend to think that allowing everyone a wide scope of personal freedom would work better than the conservative or left-wing alternatives.

Conservatives worry that libertarians fail to see the real depravity in human nature. Conservatives argue that society depends on unconscious, poorly understood rules and conventions. Traditional modes of life help maintain these rules and conventions. We often do not realize how certain traditions—such as religious commitment—are valuable until they are gone.

Conservatives worry that libertarianism undermines the underlying social order. For instance, conservatives claim the traditional family is the bedrock of society. When the family breaks down, crime, poverty, and economic stagnation are sure to follow. Many conservatives believe that to preserve the family, governments must encourage traditional marriages. Many conservatives also believe that people's moral codes will erode outside a religious culture. Because libertarianism permits experimentation and tolerates almost anything, it will destroy the traditions upon which society depends.

The Left also sees libertarians as overly optimistic about how well markets and civil society can function. For example, libertarians think private charity tends to work better than government welfare programs. Left-liberals and others on the left worry that libertarians are both too optimistic about people's willingness to contribute to these programs and too optimistic about the ability of private agencies to solve these problems. The Left believes that only government can solve the problem of poverty.

28. Are libertarians moral nihilists?

Moral nihilism holds that there are no moral truths. Morality nihilism says talk about morality is like talk about ghosts, astrology, or witches. Saying, "It's wrong to steal" is like saying, "There's a poltergeist in my shoe."

Libertarians are not nihilists. If a person had no moral commitments, she could not be a libertarian. Libertarians advocate tolerance, not because they think there are no moral truths, but because they think one of the moral truths is that we should be tolerant.

Libertarians might seem to be nihilists because they reject legal moralism. *Legal moralism* holds that if something is morally wrong, the law should prohibit it. Libertarians believe that the law ought to allow people to perform many immoral actions. For instance, libertarians say that while it's morally wrong to write racist literature, the state should allow people to do so. Or, to take another example, it would be wrong for me to break a promise to meet you for dinner, but that doesn't mean the state should force me to keep my word. We often have the right to do wrong. In many cases, even though it's wrong to do something, it's also wrong for others to stop us from doing it.

29. Is libertarianism atheistic?

Libertarianism has no conceptual connection to atheism or theism. Libertarianism is compatible with a belief in divinity, but it does not rest upon, require, or imply any such belief. Libertarianism has little more to say about religion than it has to say about chemistry.

That said, there is evidence that libertarians tend to reject supernatural beliefs. *Liberty Magazine*, a small libertarian magazine, polls its readers every 10 years. The 2008 survey indicated that only 36.5% of its readers believed in a god. In contrast, Gallup polls regularly find that over 90% of Democrats, Republicans, and independents believe in a god. *Reason*, a more popular libertarian magazine, is avowedly atheistic. Its motto is "free minds and free markets."

If libertarians are disproportionately atheistic, there is no clear reason why. One possibility is that libertarians tend to be more philosophical than others—they are more likely than conservatives or the Left to engage with philosophy or think like philosophers. Philosophers, in turn, strongly tend to be atheists. (A recent poll showed that only about 3 in 20 academic philosophers believe in a god.)

30. Are libertarians individualists?

In one sense of individualism, yes. Libertarians believe each individual human life is important. They do not regard society as an organism with a good of its own, distinct from the good of the individuals who form it. Libertarians reject the view (associated with fascism, certain versions of conservatism, and radical socialism) that individuals should be sacrificed for the benefit of society as a whole.

There's another popular definition of individualism. Individualism, in this second sense, idealizes the person who chooses her own life plan, is passionately creative, rises above the masses, and resists authority. The individualist is a rational deliberator and a reflective chooser of ends. The individualist experiments with different ways of living. The individualist's code of values is not determined by and bound up in the traditions and expectations of her culture. Many libertarians are also individualists in this sense. But many are not. Libertarianism takes no stance on what the good life is.

When many people call libertarians individualists, they mean to use the term derisively. They mean to suggest that libertarians do not care about community or about social bonds. They believe libertarians celebrate personal autonomy and deliberative self-development at the expense of love, family, or friendship or at the expense of joining clubs, churches, or causes. Conservatives believe libertarianism would tend to break down certain communities and traditions.

Suppose conservative critics of libertarianism are correct—that is, suppose that under libertarian politics, tight-knit communities would give way to atomism. Suppose solidarity would disappear. Suppose society would become a system of alienated strangers.

Many libertarians agree with conservatives that this would be lamentable. However, libertarians still do not think this would justify government invention in favor of traditional values. They oppose using state coercion as a *substitute* or *stand-in* for community.

Conservatives and left-liberals alike take this to show that libertarians have no community spirit. Libertarians find this puzzling. They ask, why would "caring about community" involve pushing others around or subjugating them to the group's will? Conservatives and left-liberals alike often think we must use violence to encourage community, perhaps by outlawing certain lifestyles or by forcing citizens to do community service or vote. Libertarians respond: If "community" requires systematic violence, what kind of community is that, and why would *that* kind of community be worth wanting? Libertarians say, if a community can flourish only in an atmosphere of oppression, then that community is no real community at all. Truly loving communities—just like loving families—do not need background threats to survive.

Many libertarians in fact think that community spirit is needed to make a free society work. They want voluntary civil society to perform many of the functions associated with the welfare state. For instance, the historian David Beito argues that in the past, mutual aid societies used to provide community health and unemployment insurance.

Workers would band together to hire lodge doctors at discounted rates.

Some critics believe private mechanisms for providing social insurance will not succeed. Private charity, private insurance, and mutual aid societies can help somewhat. However, they are no substitute for government-provided aid.

We can count on civil society to do something, but not to do enough. Or, they argue, even though private retirement investment accounts are superior to Social Security, most people will not choose to invest enough, and so the government must provide Social Security for them.

4

GOVERNMENT AND DEMOCRACY

31. How do libertarians define "government"?

By definition, the government of a society is the part of that society that (1) claims a rightful monopoly on the use of coercive force, (2) claims the right to make and impose rules on others, and (3) has the effective coercive power to enforce these claims. This is the standard definition of "government" in political philosophy.

Governments enforce their rules with violence or threats of violence. To illustrate this point, the philosopher Michael Huemer asks you to imagine you receive a speeding ticket for $100. When the government issues you a ticket, it thereby commands you to pay it $100. What happens if you do not pay? At first, the government will issue *more* commands. It will increase the fine and thus command you to pay more. It might eventually revoke your license. To revoke your license is to command you not to drive. Now, suppose you ignore all of these commands. You continue to drive as you please and you do not pay the fines. Eventually, the government will arrest and imprison you. It will command you to submit to the police. If you do not heed its command to submit, it will use violence to make you submit. If you continue to refuse its commands, it will tase you, beat you, or shoot you.

This is one reason why libertarians dislike using government to solve problems or to change people's behavior. To say, "There ought to be a law against X!" is the same thing as saying, "The government ought to threaten people with violence!" There's no getting around this issue. Whatever good or bad governments may do, governments are always and everywhere institutions of violence.

32. Why do libertarians favor limited government and dislike big government?

There are at least two different senses of "big government." Libertarians dislike big government in both senses.

By "big government" we might mean government that governs many people. Libertarians tend to believe governments suffer from *diseconomies of scale*. It's harder to govern 300 million people than 5 million. This may be one reason why Denmark and Switzerland have more competent governments than the United States.

Of course, the other sense of "big government" is *interventionist* government. A big government is a government that does many things in many areas of life. Libertarians distrust big government for three main reasons.

First, they regard governments as forms of institutionalized violence. Libertarians are averse to violence and thus dislike having government solve problems.

Second, libertarians believe government agents often have bad motives. Politicians want to serve their own good rather than the common good.

The historian Lord Acton says that power tends to corrupt, and absolute power tends to corrupt absolutely. The power to do good through government is the same as the power to do evil. When we create a CIA or SEC, we have noble goals. However, the people who seek the power we create will not always have noble intentions. The power we create to save our children will often be used against them instead.

When good people and bad people compete for power, the bad have an advantage. The good people, being good, will observe moral constraints. The bad will do whatever it takes to win.

Even when politicians mean well, they might have to subvert the rule of law to get their way. Democracies lead to disagreement, not consensus. Politicians might want to do good, but they cannot count on getting a coalition behind them. To be effective, they must often break the rules.

Civil liberties columnist Glenn Greenwald points out that before Obama (a former constitutional law scholar) was elected, he claimed, "The President does not have power under the Constitution to unilaterally authorize a military attack in a situation that does not involve stopping an actual or imminent threat to the nation." As a candidate, Obama also said, "No more ignoring the law when it's inconvenient. That is not who we are.... We will again set an example for the world that the law is not subject to the whims of stubborn rulers." Yet, as Greenwald neatly documents, President Obama ignored these claims in order to wage an illegal war in Libya. Obama ignores the rule of law whenever he can, just like his predecessor.

The dark side of limited government is that it is, after all, limited. There are things we want government to do that limited governments cannot do. The bright side of limited government is that other people with better connections than ours also seek power. A limited government limits their ability to further their aims at our expense.

Third, governments are often incompetent. Even when governments want to fix problems, there is no guarantee they will succeed. Libertarians worry that governments often make things worse, not better.

Most people, including government agents, are biased to overestimate how well their plans will go. They are biased to rush into action rather than think things through. They are biased to focus on the direct effects of their actions and to ignore the indirect, unseen, or unintended consequences.

Governments often fail to account for unintended consequences. For example, many cities impose rent controls with the goal of keeping housing affordable. Yet when apartment prices are kept artificially low, demand exceeds supply, and this creates a housing shortage.

Or, to take another example, libertarians oppose the War on Drugs in part because they think it increases violent crime. Libertarians believe the drug war forces poor inner-city African Americans to grow up in poverty and violence. Libertarians say that we didn't learn our lessons from the War on Alcohol. Prohibition created a black market in alcohol, empowered the mafia, and produced heavy gang violence.

As a final example, libertarians oppose centrally planned economies in part because central planners cannot acquire the information they need to plan effectively. In market economies, prices convey information about supply and demand. Market prices tell businesses, workers, and others what they need to do to serve others' needs. Centrally planned economies have no workable substitute for market prices. Thus, central planners have to guess. They usually guess wrongly. Soviet Russia had a low standard of living throughout its history.

Libertarians say this also explains why government interventions in a mixed economy also often fail. Governments do not and cannot have the information they need. Knowledge is often dispersed and local. There is often no way to communicate that knowledge to a central regulatory committee.

33. Are libertarians anarchists?

Many are, but many are not.

Anarchists believe we should dispense with government. (See question 31 for a definition of "government.") Anarchism is the rejection of statism. Statists advocate having some sort of government. Almost everyone alive today is a statist so defined.

An "anarchist," in this sense, does not advocate chaos or disorder. Anarchist libertarians do not think anarchy would be a chaotic disaster. Instead, they believe that people can live together in a more prosperous and just way without government than with it, despite all the flaws in human nature. Actually, most anarchist libertarians believe anarchism is preferable to statism *because* of the flaws in human nature. A typical person believes anarchy would be preferable to statism, if only human beings were angels. Anarchists believe statism would be preferable to anarchy, if only human beings were angels. Libertarian anarchism might seem utopian to everyone else. Yet libertarian anarchists argue that statism is utopian. Most states throughout history have been disastrous for human rights. The best states we've produced so far are still pretty bad.

Libertarian anarchists believe that it is dangerous to give anyone a monopoly on rule-making authority and coercive power. As the legal theorist John Hasnas says, "Libertarian anarchists are just people who take anti-trust seriously." That is, your reasons to stop Wal-Mart from becoming a monopoly are even stronger reasons to avoid a monopoly on coercive power.

Some libertarian anarchists prefer systems of "polycentric law." In polycentric law, there are multiple providers of law, which compete for customers in a given area. These providers offer their own legal rules, and individuals may choose which system to accept. When conflicts arise between different centers of law, the centers will want to avoid expensive violent conflict and will instead use arbitration. Polycentric law avoids central planning and instead relies upon decentralized negotiation and bargaining.

Many on the left now favor "deliberative democracy." Deliberative democrats are statists. They want to impose one law upon all. However, they do not want to decide laws through adversarial contests, such as elections. They prefer that people deliberate together and reach consensus about politics.

Libertarian anarchists say we can have real deliberation and consensus only if we avoid monopolistic laws. If no person has the power to bend everyone else to his will, then the only choice is to find common ground.

You might think this polycentric legal system would barely function. On the contrary, some of the best laws we have actually did evolve within a system of polycentric law. In common law countries, such as the United States, England, Canada, and Australia, commercial law, merchant law, property law, and tort law actually did evolve in a polycentric legal system, often completely outside of and without any backing from government. These laws regulated commercial activity for hundreds of years and were only later adopted by governments. For instance, the *lex mercatoria*—merchant law—was developed and administered by merchant courts (which lacked governmental enforcement powers) rather than by government courts.

Today, we are accustomed to living in nation-states. We thus tend to assume that effective laws can exist only if governments create and enforce them. However, this assumption is historically inaccurate. In fact, most of our laws did not originally come from governments, and for a long time functioned effectively without government support.

In medieval England, the king, the lords, and the church each ran their own competing courts. Disputants could bring their disputes to any of these courts. The courts made money by getting the reputation for making the best decisions. Both parties to the dispute wanted to win, but they also shared a common interest in finding a court that could reach a decision they both could live with. Or, even today, our own societies have elements of polycentric law. Universities, shopping centers, homeowners associations, and others make rules that often conflict with and bypass the state's legal order.

34. Do libertarians believe there is a duty to obey the law?

Libertarians think a law is just a law. There are good laws and bad laws, just and unjust laws. The mere fact that something is a law tells us *nothing* at all about whether we should obey it.

In the United States, it was once illegal to send literature about contraception through the mail. The United States used to require Americans to turn in escaped slaves. Many parts of the United States used to criminalize sex between blacks and whites. Nazi Germany used to require its citizens to mistreat Jews. The United Kingdom chemically castrated mathematician Alan Turing for having sex with another man. These and many other laws are vile, libertarians say, and no person should obey them.

Libertarians believe in a presumption of liberty. (See question 21.) They thus presume that all laws are *unjust, illegitimate, and lacking in authority* until shown otherwise. For any law, the default assumption is that I do not have to obey it. It is always an open question whether any government has the right to enforce its rules. It is always an open question whether anyone has a duty to obey a law.

Note that saying we have no duty to obey the law is not the same as saying we may do anything we please.

For instance, libertarians agree we should not murder each other. But the reason I shouldn't murder you is because murder is morally wrong. It's not wrong because the government says so. Even if the government legalized murder, it would still be wrong to murder people. So, when a libertarian says there's no duty to obey the law prohibiting murder, she's not saying that it's okay for people to kill each other.

Or consider that in the United States, we drive on the right rather than the left. Libertarians agree that we should observe these conventions. We should observe certain necessary social conventions in order to avoid endangering and harming other people. The fact that some social conventions are enshrined in law is incidental. Suppose the United States didn't have any such laws, but everyone still drove on the right. We'd have just as much obligation to drive on the right.

35. Do libertarians think politicians are selfish and evil?

Libertarians view politics without romance. People are people. Joining the government does not transform sinners into saints.

In contrast, most people have a romantic view of government. They view government as the leadership of a big national club. They associate working in government with civic virtue and public-spiritedness. They tend to believe the politicians on their side, at least, are unusually good people.

Libertarians agree that many politicians mean well. Libertarians say the problem is that many well-meaning, public-spirited people have false beliefs about how to make the world better. For instance, the economist Bryan Caplan, the legal theorist Ilya Somin, and I argue that typical voters are well intentioned but grossly irrational about politics. Voters are like quack doctors who want to cure pneumonia using leeches instead of penicillin. They are terrible at picking leaders who know more than they themselves do. Instead, voters pick politicians who share their misconceptions. The politician who wins the election is whoever appeals most to the median voter. The median voter would fail ECON 101. Thus, the typical congressperson advocates counterproductive policies.

Politicians overspend, but this need not reflect malice or self-interest. Congress may simply have a culture of spending. Most people who lobby Congress ask for *more* spending rather then less spending. This is not surprising. The benefits of spending are concentrated among the few, but the costs are diffused among the many. If your corporation can get millions in subsidies, your corporation will spend time and money to get that subsidy. The cost of the subsidy is spread among all taxpayers. It costs the typical taxpayer only a few dollars on average. Taxpayers thus have no incentive to fight the subsidy or even to know about it. Lobbying *for* spending pays for itself; lobbying *against* spending costs more than it saves.

In light of all this, imagine you are a congressperson. You hear many cries for help. These cries for help only come in the form of spending requests. No one ever asks you not to spend. It is easy to believe you hurt no one by spending. The victims of overspending are unseen.

So, contrary to the stereotype, libertarians do not believe all politicians are selfish. Libertarians often think that politicians are inept, counterproductive do-gooders.

Still, the stereotype is partly right. Libertarians do believe government tends to attract bad people.

Libertarians believe that in politics, the worst often get on top. Political power can be used for good or for bad. When people compete for this power, the virtuous observe moral constraints, but the vicious will do whatever it takes.

Libertarians believe power tends to corrupt—it corrupts both the people who hold it and the people subject to it. We are biased to view political power as majestic. We tie esteem to political power. We thus allow kings, emperors, presidents, senators, district attorneys, police officers, and even voters to commit injustice.

For example, many Americans would rate Abraham Lincoln as the greatest president. Yet Lincoln fought the civil war not to free slaves, but to force the South to remain part of the United States. In the course of war, Lincoln suppressed habeas corpus, created the first national draft, suppressed free speech, censored and punished newspapers editors who criticized his war efforts, and was at least complicit in waging total war against innocent Southern civilians. By normal moral standards, this makes him a monster. (If I did these things, you would regard me as a vile and despicable person.) However, we rarely judge political leaders by normal moral standards—we hold them to much lower standards than normal. As the historian Lord Acton said, "Great men are nearly always bad men."

Political power encourages hubris. There are few thoughts more corrupting than, "This goal is so important that I will do whatever it takes." Leaders often view themselves as exempt from normal moral rules.

Deep disagreement is normal in democratic government. We do not all agree about facts or values. Deliberation and discussion do not resolve all our disputes. Do-gooders can rarely get consensus to do good. Thus, to do good in a democratic government, do-gooders must often subvert the democratic process and the rule of law. Thus, libertarians are not surprised to see that as president, Obama abuses power just as much as George W. Bush did.

36. What is government failure and how does it relate to market failure?

In economic theory, government failure is the political counterpart to market failure.

A market failure occurs whenever markets produce a less than perfectly efficient allocation of goods and services. A government failure occurs whenever government produces a less than perfectly efficient allocation of goods and services. In the real world, neither governments nor markets are perfectly efficient, and so all government and markets "fail" all the time. Of course, most market or government "failures," so defined, are not disasters.

Critics accuse libertarians of ignoring market failures. Critics say libertarians believe markets solve everything. Some libertarians think this way, but most do not. Most libertarians are not market zealots.

Instead, libertarians think both markets and governments fail badly. Libertarians think that once we account for both market *and* government failures, this heavily favors markets over governments. As the Nobel laureate libertarian economist Gary Becker says, "...on the whole, government failure is far more pervasive, damaging, and less self-correcting, than is market failure." He thus recommends government intervention only in cases where market failures are serious and persistent. The general presumption should be in favor of markets.

In real markets, agents make bad choices. They are often ignorant, misinformed, and irrational. Yet, markets tend to punish agents for making bad choices, and they tend to learn from their mistakes. For instance, if you fail to pay your bills, your credit rating declines and you have a harder time getting loans. If you fail to do research and buy an unreliable car, you suffer from repair bills.

In contrast, when people in government make bad choices, the political process almost never punishes them. Studies show that voters are terrible at retrospective voting—they do not know whom to blame for bad government—and so politicians are not punished for making bad choices. Or, consider that the probability that an individual vote will affect the outcome of an election is vanishingly small. A voter is more likely to win Powerball a few times in a row than to change the outcome of an election. Thus, individual voters are not punished for making bad choices or rewarded for making good choices. Political agents rarely learn from their mistakes. Government failures are less self-correcting than market failures.

The typical undergraduate microeconomics textbook describes cases where markets are unlikely to produce efficient outcomes. These textbooks often claim that, in principle, government intervention could solve the market failure.

However, these textbooks also assume that government both (1) has full information about how to solve the problem and (2) has the good faith to use its power to solve the problem.

It is as if the textbooks say omniscient angels can intervene to solve market failures. Thus, when undergraduate textbooks recommend government intervention, they mean intervention by *idealized* governments, not necessarily by *real* governments. In the real world, libertarians believe, sometimes the best response to serious market failure is just to suck it up and live with it.

Sophisticated anti-libertarians and sophisticated libertarians can thus be seen as having an empirical dispute. Libertarians think the balance of market successes versus government successes, and market failures versus government failures, favors free markets over government intervention. Anti-libertarians think the balance comes out the other way. In principle, this dispute can be resolved by empirical data.

37. What are some forms of government failure?

1. Governments fail through *over*regulation. Some regulations have no real benefit—they just waste money and make innovation harder. Other regulations save lives, but at too high a cost.

In a famous study, Tammy Tengs and her colleagues (none of whom are libertarian, for what that's worth) measured the cost-effectiveness of 587 regulations. They found great variation. The Federal Aviation Administration's regulations cost, on average, $23,000 to extend one person's life one year. The Environmental Protection Agency's regulations average $7.6 million per life-year extended.

The costs of overregulation are often unseen. Suppose we insist that drugs are proven perfectly safe and effective before we allow them on the market. Regulating medicine causes *drug lag* and *drug loss*. "Drug lag" refers to the time needed to get a drug approved. In the United States, average drug lag is over 12 years. In that time, people suffer or die from whatever the drugs would cure. "Drug loss" refers to how regulations prevent useful drugs from being developed or coming to the market. It costs over $1 billion on average in the United States to bring a drug to market. This means that drug companies will only pursue highly profitable drugs with wide appeal (such as drugs for erectile dysfunction) rather than less profitable drugs with narrow appeal. It also means drug companies will not make drugs that only help the poor.

Sophisticated defenders of the FDA acknowledge these costs. They just claim that the benefits of FDA drug regulation exceed these costs.

2. Governments fail by *mis*regulating. Sometimes governments just make bad choices. For instance, the Federal Reserve is supposed to stabilize the economy and banking system by controlling the money supply. It is also supposed to prevent bank insolvency by being a lender of last resort. Some classical and neoclassical liberals believe the Federal Reserve System is needed to keep the supply and demand for money in equilibrium. Others believe the Federal Reserve makes things worse. For instance, the economist George Selgin argues that after the creation of the Fed, US banking became more unstable, not less. Also, the Federal Reserve is supposed to be independent, but politicians often sway the Fed to do their bidding. For instance, President Nixon pushed the Fed to stimulate the economy right before the 1972 election. This created a short-term boom with a longer-term bust, but it helped Nixon win re-election.

Many critics of libertarianism believe that free markets in banking lead to depressions and massive bank failures. They cite the numerous bank failures and runs on banks in the late nineteenth century in the United States as evidence. However, libertarian economists argue that in the late 1800s, the United States did not have an unregulated free market in banking. Instead, banks were regulated in ways that forced them to accept undue risk and that made banking more volatile. For instance, the government did not allow banks to form branches in different markets, which would have allowed the banks to spread risk by using one market to insure others. Banks were required to accept bad local and state government debts as collateral. During the Great Depression, the United States had thousands of bank failures, despite having a central bank. Canada had no central bank and yet had zero bank failures. Canada's banking system has always been freer than the United States', and has always been more stable.

3. Governments fail by enabling *rent seeking*. "Rent seeking" is a fancy word for cronyism and pork barrel politics. An individual, firm, or union engages in rent seeking when it tries to change the laws or regulations, or how the laws and regulations are administered, in order to secure a special benefit for itself. Rent seekers try to get the government to manipulate the market in their favor.

Big corporations want to make money, but making money on the free market is hard. You have to be better than your competitors. Making money by rigging the rules is easier. You just need to have better connections. When well-meaning voters and politicians create government power in order to control and restrain corporations, corporations often capture this very power. When we attempt to control corporate power through government, we often instead end up *giving* corporations even more power.

Firms sometimes lobby the government to impose certain regulations or taxes on their industry, because they expect these regulations or taxes will harm the firm's competitors more. (For instance, Amazon wants an Internet sales tax in order to hurt eBay.) Or, a firm might lobby for a subsidy, tariff, or trade barrier. Subsidies lower the firm's costs, while tariffs and trade barriers reduce competition. Or, a firm might try to socialize its risks, such as when a bank induces a government to bail out bad loans. Or, a firm might induce the government to grant it monopoly status, so that it has no competitors at all.

Rent seeking is costly and destructive. Some economists estimate rent seeking destroys 3% of the US gross national product (GNP). Others think it destroys as much as 50% of the US GNP. Most estimate the total losses as somewhere in the middle. If they are right, then rent seeking destroys trillions of dollars.

Rent seeking is destructive in part because it stifles innovation. In rent-seeking societies, firms depend on government favor. They spend money and time on seeking favors rather than innovating. The cost of entry into the market grows too high, so that only large, privileged corporations remain.

4. Government can also fail by creating perverse incentives. As an example, the ecologist Richard Stroup tells the story of Ben Cone. Ben Cone inherited 7,200 acres of forest in 1982. He used the forest as a wildlife reserve and for old growth timber, cutting a little at a time. His environmentally friendly management technique encouraged an endangered species of woodpecker to nest in some of his trees. The Endangered Species Act required him to cordon off a large circle of land around the woodpecker nests. When Cone learned of this regulation, he began clear-cutting the remaining forest. (He could not afford to let the birds spread to the rest of his land.) The Endangered Species Act punished environmentally friendly behavior.

Or, to take another example, many governments bind themselves to the Basel Accords, a set of international standards for banking laws and regulations. The Basel Accords try to prevent banking collapses by setting reserve ratios and managing lending risk. Basel tells private banks to treat government debt as risk free. But government debt is not risk free. The European banks that followed the Basel Accords now have too much exposure to bad Greek, Portuguese, and Italian debt. (As I write, this may yet cause a massive European recession.)

5. Governments might also fail because of diseconomies of scale. A political system designed to govern 4 million people (the approximate US population in 1789) might fail at governing 310 million people (the approximate US population right now). Denmark and Switzerland may have better and more

competent government than the United States in part because they govern fewer people.

38. Do libertarians favor democracy?

Most libertarians believe democracy is superior to other forms of government.

However, libertarians do not valorize democracy. They do not regard democracy as an end in itself. They do not regard democratic participation and deliberation as the highest form of life. They tend to believe that democracy, like all forms of government, is inherently repugnant. In a democracy, the people do not literally govern themselves. Rather, a subset of people takes itself to have the right to order other people around and to force others to do things they do not want to do.

In Western democracies, when we exalt democracies, what we exalt is *constitutional* democracy. The constitutional part is more important than the democracy part. To be worth defending, democracy has to be limited. There are things our neighbors must not be allowed to do, even if they can muster a large voting majority. As classicist and philosopher Paul Woodruff says, "The tyranny of the majority kills freedom as dead as any other form of tyranny. It's not freedom if you have to join the majority in order to feel that you are free."

Many nonlibertarians have an almost religious reverence for democracy. They love democracy so much that they wish to see democracy in every aspect of life. They want democracy to be a way of living. They want everything open to democratic deliberation and decision making.

Libertarians instead want to insulate people from political control. They do not want every decision to be subject to discussion. They believe one of the greatest freedoms of all is not having to justify yourself to others. If your entire life resembles a committee meeting, you are not free.

Libertarians favor giving everyone an extensive sphere of civil and economic liberty. (See questions 22, 45, and 62.) However,

libertarians usually do not believe that the political liberties—
the rights to run for office, hold positions of power, or vote—
are the same kind of thing as the civil and economic liberties.
When I have a right of free speech, that gives me power over
myself. But if I have the right to vote, that gives me power over
others. The right to vote is a partial right to rule other people.

Libertarians tend to favor democracy for instrumental reasons. Democracy has a better track record compared to other
forms of government. Democracies tend to respect citizens'
liberties more. Democracies are on average less warmonger-
ing and imperialistic.

Still, many libertarians say, democracy's track record is
poor. Consider the United States. Right before World War II
began, the libertarian essayist Alford Jay Nock said:

> [I]n order to keep down the great American sin of self-
> righteousness, every public presentation ought to draw
> the deadly parallel with the record of the American
> State. The German State is persecuting a minority, just
> as the American State did after 1776; the Italian State
> breaks into Ethiopia, just as the American State broke
> into Mexico; the Japanese State kills off the Manchurian
> tribes in wholesale lots, just as the American State did
> the Indian tribes; the British State practices large-scale
> carpetbaggery, like the American State after 1864; the
> imperialist French State massacres native civilians on
> their own soil, as the American State did in pursuit of its
> imperialistic policies in the Pacific, and so on.

Throughout history, and right now, Western democracies
routinely abuse their citizens, trample the rights of noncitizens,
and wage unjust wars. The United States and United Kingdom
had imperialist policies throughout the nineteenth and early
twentieth centuries. (Some would say that the United States
continues to have imperialist policies today.) When American

diplomats condemned the Nazi treatment of Jews, the Nazis pointed to how the United States treated blacks and asked, "Who are you to talk?"

Libertarians thus have only a weak fondness for democracy. Some anti-libertarians take this as evidence that libertarianism is, in some way, asocial. They think the best society would be one where everyone comes together as equals and decides collectively the best way to live.

39. Why do some libertarians say democracies make dumb choices?

Imagine your friend Bob wants to lose weight, but has bizarre beliefs about how to do so. Bob believes that to lose weight, he must avoid exercise and eat 100 Oreos per day. Bob might have good intentions, but he does not know what he is doing.

Many libertarians—and many nonlibertarians—think that when it comes to politics, the median American voter is much like Bob. Voters tend to have good intentions but are badly informed, misinformed, and even irrational about politics.

In the 1950s, University of Michigan researchers began measuring Americans' political knowledge. They found that most Americans are ignorant about basic civics. They cannot identify their representatives. They do not know what the different branches of government do. They cannot identify which political party is more conservative.

More recently, economists, psychologists, and political scientists started to study political *rationality*. They find that most people suffer from cognitive biases. Cognitive biases are systematic deviations from rational thought. Biases are like software bugs in the brain. They prevent us from believing, thinking, or doing what we should, given the information we have. For instance, in political thinking, we are overly optimistic about our plans. We dismiss and ignore evidence that would undermine our current beliefs. We are biased to do something rather than do nothing. The economist Bryan Caplan and legal theorist Ilya Somin, among others, argue that voters have systematically false beliefs about basic, textbook economics and political science. Voters do not merely know nothing—they know *less* than nothing.

The (nonlibertarian) psychologists David Dunning and John Kruger have argued that "incompetent people are inherently unable to judge the competence of other people, or the quality of other people's ideas." If voters have systematic false beliefs—such as a systematic distrust of foreign trade—then we get bad government as a result. Voters not only are systematically mistaken about basic economics, but they cannot figure out which candidates know more than they do. So, for instance, voters are not only bad at estimating the effects of free trade on the economy but also bad at determining which candidates are better at making such estimates. Thus, in democracy, incompetent leaders with false beliefs win. Libertarians say: If the candidates seem clueless, it is because the system works.

Politics is high stakes. Choosing the wrong leaders can cause war or economic depression. Yet individual voters have little incentive to be well informed or rational. An individual vote has impact only if it changes the outcome of the election. (Some might claim that an individual vote might "change the mandate," but political scientists have shown there is no such thing as a mandate that increases political effectiveness.) Yet, an individual vote has almost no chance of changing the outcome of any major election. Thus, even in a high-stakes election, and even if you care about everyone else's welfare, it is not worth the cost to try to become better informed or to become more scrupulously rational.

This is one reason why libertarians want to limit democratic power. If voters were well informed and highly rational, we might want democracies to have a broad scope of power. But if voters are ignorant and irrational, then we will want to trust them with far less power.

40. What do libertarians think about the US Constitution?

Libertarians want a constitutional government with sharply delimited powers. The less angelic or competent our leaders are, the less discretionary power we want our leaders to have.

Written constitutions contain legal guarantees, but legal guarantees guarantee nothing. To maintain a constitutional regime, citizens must be strongly committed to maintaining a constitutional regime. Some forms of government make it easier to undermine or bypass commitment. But written constitutions are not self-enforcing.

The worst dictatorships and totalitarian regimes have often had liberal written constitutions, constitutions indistinguishable from those in liberal Western democracies. For instance, the Soviet Union under Stalin was a humanitarian disaster— most scholars estimate Stalin's government killed more than 20 million people (outside of war)—even though the USSR's constitution guaranteed human rights.

Libertarians are glad that the US Constitution legally limits the governments' power. They are glad that it separates government powers and so, to that extent, tends to slow down the lawmaking process. They are glad that the Bill of Rights lists a wide range of liberties.

However, the US Constitution is just paper. Libertarians might say, Do you like the idea of separation of powers? Watch it disappear: Congress has authorized the president to decide when and how to go to war. Do you like the right of free speech and freedom of the press guaranteed by the First Amendment? For most of American history, the US Supreme Court did not forbid censorship. Think it is important that governments respect habeas corpus? (Habeas corpus is the principle that governments must not imprison or detain people without trial or evidence.) Lincoln suspended it during the Civil War. The Supreme Court demanded he respect habeas corpus. Lincoln ignored the Supreme Court with impunity.

There is nothing magic about the US Constitution. As I write, Congress and the president authorized the US military to detain anyone anywhere indefinitely without charge or trial, provided the person "substantially supports" certain terrorist groups. As I write, Obama asserts the right to assassinate American citizens without trial.

If you want to see proof that the Constitution is not self-enforcing, just watch a confirmation hearing when the President nominates a justice to serve on the Supreme Court. Supreme Court justices do not interpret the Constitution objectively or disinterestedly, but instead "interpret" so that the Constitution generates their preferred political result. Conservative justices "interpret" the Constitution as requiring conservatism. Liberal justices "interpret" the Constitution as requiring liberalism. Senators know all this, of course. Thus, liberal senators try to block conservative justices, while conservative justices try to block liberal justices. Supreme Court confirmation hearings are political battles—fights over what future law will be, rather than evaluations of nominee's real merit. If the Supreme Court were objective, you would not be able to predict how a justice will decide a case just by determining justices' political preferences.

The Articles of Confederation were the original government documents of the United States. The actual—indeed, intended—effect of replacing the Articles of Confederation with the Constitution was not to protect liberty or promote social justice, but to *strengthen* the central government. The Constitution gave the central government the power to tax, to raise and maintain an army, and to regulate commerce.

Shay's Rebellion in 1786 prompted many leaders to replace the Articles of Confederation and to favor a stronger central government. Daniel Shay was an honored and decorated soldier during the American Revolutionary War. Like many revolutionary soldiers, Shay was never paid for his service. He returned from service with large farm debts—debts he could not pay because he was not paid for his military service.

European creditors wanted payment in gold and silver, but these were in short supply. Shay and other badly treated veterans worried their property would be confiscated and they would be placed in debtors' prisons. They petitioned the Massachusetts government to fix the problem. Boston ignored their petitions. Finally, in desperation, Shay and other farmers rebelled. They formed a militia to prevent local courts from confiscating their property. Under the Articles of Confederation, it was difficult for the US central government to help Massachusetts crush the rebellion.

American public school history books tell the story of Shay's Rebellion in order to show that the US Constitution was necessary. Some libertarians take an alternative reading: The government treated Shay and his fellow farmers in an extremely unjust way. If Shay's Rebellion is supposed to justify the US Constitution, what is the justification, that the Constitution makes it easier for the government to oppress the poor? At any rate, the main purpose of the US Constitution was not to protect liberty, but to empower the federal government.

41. Are libertarians nationalists?

Nationalists believe that the fact that we are citizens of different nation-states is morally important. They think we owe more to our fellow citizens than we owe to others.

Most people tend to think that in our daily lives, we may show some special preferences for our children, friends, or family members. For example, commonsense morality holds that I may give my kids birthday presents instead of spending that money to save distant strangers' children from starving.

In effect, nationalism is the view that we should treat all the members of our nation-states as part of an extended family. If nationalism were true, then this would explains why, for example, Sweden may spend huge sums promoting the welfare of its quite wealthy "lower" classes while more or less ignoring the real suffering of the world's desperate poor. Or, if more extreme forms of nationalism were true, then it would explain why governments may kill, exploit, or impoverish innocent civilians of other countries to benefit their own citizens, even when the costs to foreign citizens greatly exceeds the benefits to their own citizens.

Libertarians oppose nationalism. Libertarians believe that membership in a nation-state is, in some sense, morally arbitrary. Domestic governments must not treat the citizens of foreign nations as if their lives were less valuable. This in part explains why libertarians oppose war and favor open immigration.

Libertarians deny we have special ties to our fellow citizens the way we have special ties to friends and family. Other citizens are *strangers*. I have no special connection to people in California as opposed to Ontario.

One common argument for nationalism asserts that each of us owes a debt to society. In the state of nature, outside of civil society, life would be solitary, nasty, poor, brutish, and short. However, because I live in civil society, my life is pleasant, rich, civil, and long. I was educated in New Hampshire schools. I now drive on roads provided by Virginia and Washington, DC. I make purchases with American money. I am as rich as I am because I benefit from the past behavior of other Americans. So, the argument goes, I thus owe a debt to New Hampshire, Virginia, or the United States.

Libertarians think the "debt to society" argument fails to justify nationalism. If I owe some society a debt, there is no reason to think I specially owe *America* a debt. I benefited from public education, but why think that indebts me to *America* rather than Hudson, New Hampshire? I benefit from the positive externalities created by an extensive system of trade, but why think that indebts me to *America* rather than the entire world?

42. How do libertarians propose to keep money out of politics?

Libertarians joke that the more important question is how to keep politics out of money.

Libertarians say the best way to keep money out of politics is to make it so that politics has little worth buying. When governments have the power to rig the economy, create winners and losers, and rob Peter to pay Paul, people will compete to control that power. Interventionist governments are like supermarkets selling favors. To reduce corruption, we must reduce the state's ability to distribute favors.

Some say that if the government regulates campaign expenditures, it can then prevent unscrupulous corporations and unions from buying politicians. Libertarians say this strategy will backfire. Trying to regulate the effect of money on politics might increase the effect of money on politics. After all, any agency with the power to regulate campaign spending is itself a prime target for institutional capture. A corporation would love to have the FDA in its pocket. But if it can put the FEC in its pocket, even better.

Most Americans believe that money buys elections. They believe that when donors give money to politicians, the donors thereby purchase friendly political policies. Big donors decide what politicians do.

To laypeople, all this seems obviously true, yet the political scientists who study this issue (and, for what it's worth, also tend to lean left, reject libertarianism, and vote Democrat) generally believe this is all false. For decades, political scientists have tried and failed to demonstrate that campaign spending decides electoral outcomes and laws. The belief that money buys elections is just a popular myth. The evidence does not support the belief.

Political scientists instead believe campaign spending is a "consumption good." Donors want to be part of the winning team. Campaign spending does not *make* winners; it *chases* them. Winners do not win because they raise more money. They raise more money because they are going to win.

In *Citizens United v. Federal Election Commission* (2010), the US Supreme Court decided that corporations and individuals could spend as much money as they pleased on political advertising and political communication. Many on the left in the United States were outraged, thinking this would allow rich corporations to buy electoral results with advertising. However, this folk belief contradicts the consensus of their fellow left-leaning, progressive, Democratic-voting political scientists, who have studied money and elections in depth.

In fact, there is very little money in politics. In the 2008 US federal elections, presidential candidates raised nearly $2 billion. They spent more than $1 billion. Congressional campaigns spent another one-third of a billion. Let's round up: Assume candidates and PACs spend $2.5 billion total during every presidential election. That might seem like a huge sum, but it's not. Consider that the federal government spent about $2.9 *trillion* in 2008. Campaign spending is less than one-tenth of a percent of the federal budget. Percentage-wise, that's a *tiny* amount spent to control so much power and such a huge budget. (Note also that the budget could be much bigger than it is. Candidates—and their corporate supporters—are competing to control not just the current federal budget but also the *potential* budget.) Compare: In 2008, Nike had an operating budget of about $7 billion and global revenues of about $15 billion. Yet Nike spent between $2.5 billion and $3 billion in advertising and marketing. In other words, total campaign spending in the United States, during one of the most intense election seasons ever, was about equal to Nike's marketing budget. If campaign spending really did buy laws and regulations, we would expect spending to be at least an order of magnitude higher.

43. Are libertarians doves or hawks on foreign policy?

Most libertarians are doves. They advocate peace, and mean it. American libertarians reject having the United States act as the "world's policeman."

Adam Smith's *Wealth of Nations* was in large part a critique of imperialism. We often associate opposition to imperialism with Marxism and the Left, but Smith was an outspoken critic of imperialism long before Marx. Smith said, "The rulers of Great Britain have…amused the people with imagination that they possessed a great empire on the west side of the Atlantic." In fact, Smith showed, for most English subjects, this empire was net economic loss. The British Empire enriched a few merchants, a few government officials, some arms makers, and almost no one else. Smith found the idea of empire morally revolting, but he made his case in economic terms. Using the best available data, he showed that the costs of the empire greatly exceeded the benefits. The government spent more to maintain the empire than the value of the raw materials it received from having an empire.

The economist Bryan Caplan argues that commonsense moral ideas lead to something close to pacificism. That is, in the real world, we should almost always oppose war and trying to solve problems with our military.

First, Caplan says, the immediate costs of war are high. War causes great destruction. In any major war, soldiers murder and rape civilians. Civilians see their homes, farms, and businesses destroyed. Even the winning side faces immediate costs. If a government spends $500 billion on bombs, taxpayers lose $500 billion in real wealth. To the extent we covert plowshares to swords, we don't eat.

Caplan says that all this could be justified, perhaps, if the long-run benefits of war *greatly* exceeded the immediate costs. However, he says, the long-run consequences of war are highly uncertain at best. We cannot predict how well war will go. When we think it will go well, we are almost always wrong. We are biased to be overconfident about our prospects—that is, people systematically overestimate the benefits of war and underestimate the costs. Looking back, Caplan argues, almost every war every country has fought was a mistake. When we consider fighting a new war, we are tempted to believe this war is an exception to the rule. But this belief is itself unexceptional.

Libertarians have another reason to oppose interventionist foreign policy. The economic historian Robert Higgs argues that war is the health of the state. War helps governments seize power through what Higgs calls the "ratchet effect." When a country goes to war, its government declares an emergency and seizes new massive new powers. (For instance, during the American Civil War, Lincoln suspended habeas corpus, censored and imprisoned war protestors, instituted a national draft, and instituted a national income tax.) When the war ends, the government rolls back some, but not all, of its new-found powers. It rolls back some, but not all, of its newly created bureaucracies. With each successive war, a government ratchets up its power, little by little.

5

CIVIL RIGHTS

44. What is the libertarian view of civil liberty?

Libertarians joke: Most people are libertarian toward those they regard as their equals; they are paternalistic toward those they care about but view as lower status; and they are authoritarian toward those they despise. In contrast, libertarians are libertarian toward everyone.

Throughout history, almost everyone has wanted the state to enforce virtue among citizens. Almost everyone everywhere wanted the state to impose uniform culture and religion for the sake of stability and community. Most want the state to stop people from making imprudent choices.

Some people believe we should all live in godly communities that punish sin and reward faith. Others believe we should live in societies in which no one offends the weak and marginalized. Others believe we should only eat the healthiest foods and never watch stultifying television. Others think we must not be allowed to drink alcohol, use recreational drugs, buy sex, or gamble. Most people think some such goals like these are so noble that they are willing to use violence to achieve them.

Libertarianism advocates tolerance. It is thus a demanding doctrine. It asks people to rise above normal human nature. Most of us are moral busybodies who want to control how others live. The libertarian says, "Live and let live."

Libertarians believe that everyone is sovereign over herself. How we lead our lives is up to us, so long as we respect others' rights. We are free to make stupid, imprudent, or even immoral decisions. We are free to experiment with new ways of living. We are free to join religious communities or to mock and deride religion. We are free to write patriotic songs or to burn flags. We are free to lead lives of moral virtue or vice. We are free to be prudes or to perform sex acts others find perverted.

Libertarians think that attempting to enforce prudence, virtue, or community through government tends to fail. For example, if a religious community persists only by forbidding disagreement, the community is sham.

In a free society, everyone has the right to offend others. A society in which no one has the right to offend others is itself offensive. Libertarians add: Giving everyone a right never to be offended might seem like a recipe for good community and fellow-feeling. Not so. It makes each person's sense of indignation a weapon.

45. What civil rights do libertarians think we have?

Civil liberties or civil rights are rights against interference in how we live or associate with others. The civil liberties include the right to free speech, the right of free assembly, the right of association, freedom of conscience, the right of bodily integrity and freedom from abuse and assault, freedom of lifestyle choice, the right to protest, the right to exit (i.e., the right to leave a country and to renounce citizenship), and freedom of sexual choice.

Libertarians also advocate liberal procedural rights in the criminal justice system, including the right against unwarranted search and seizure, the right to a fair trial, the right to be presumed innocent until proven guilty, the right to an expeditious trial, the right to hear one's accusers, and the right to habeas corpus. Libertarians generally oppose the death penalty and harsh criminal justice measures.

Libertarians advocate equal protection for homosexuals, and thus support same-sex marriage and oppose the US military's former restrictions on homosexuality.

Libertarians advocate women's reproductive freedom, including the rights to abortion, to birth control, and to have sex with other consenting adults.

Libertarians oppose censorship, including Internet censorship, restrictions on pornography (provided the pornographic models are consenting adults), and restrictions on flag burning or government sedition.

Unlike most conservatives and even most liberals, libertarians believe that people have the right to use drugs and make self-destructive choices. Libertarians oppose compulsory national service and the draft. Libertarians oppose the Patriot Act and government spying on Americans.

Libertarians also support free immigration. They believe people have a right to cross borders as they see fit. They hold that a Mexican has the same right to live in the United States as a native-born American. They believe everyone has the right to take employment in any other country, regardless of citizenship. They hold that, except in special circumstances, governments may not forbid citizens from leaving a country, nor may governments forbid foreigners from entering.

Some anti-libertarians think libertarians have too expansive a view of civil liberties. Others say that the question of what civil liberties we have ought to be decided politically. For instance, the legal theorist Jeremy Waldron argues that the scope of civil liberty is a contentious issue. He thinks we each have a basic right to have a say in deciding what everyone's rights should be. The libertarian view of civil liberty is just one view among many, and there's no reason why libertarians should get to impose their expansive view of civil liberties on other people if most of them favor a less expansive view.

46. What is the libertarian view of free speech and freedom of conscience?

Libertarians support strong rights of free speech and freedom of conscience. No one should be conscripted into any belief system or punished for holding unpopular beliefs. Everyone has the right to challenge or reject any other belief or opinion held by anyone else, even if that person holds that belief sacred.

Libertarians oppose government censorship of the Internet, print media, and advertisements. They believe citizens have the right to view and consume pornography (except for child pornography, because children cannot consent to sexual acts). They believe we must allow people to consume movies or video games that simulate violence. They believe we must tolerate magazines that mock cherished cultural norms. They believe we must tolerate writings that advocate sedition or terrorism. For instance, while Bin Laden didn't have the right to kill people on 9/11, he had the right to say he had the right to kill them.

This does not mean libertarians believe a person has the right to say anything she wants any time, anywhere. The right to free speech does not include the right to shout obscenities in someone else's house, uninvited, at 3 o'clock in the morning. It does not include the right to commit fraud. It does not include the right to incite a riot. It does not include the right to publish other people's Internet passwords or bank account information. Determining the exact extent of the right to free speech is philosophically complicated. But the important point here is that libertarians interpret the right of free speech as having extensive scope and heavy weight.

The American Constitution has a remarkably libertarian view of free speech. As (conservative) Chief Justice Roberts said in *United States v. Stevens* (2010), "The First Amendment's guarantee of free speech does not extend only to categories of speech that survive an ad hoc balancing of relative social costs and benefits.... Our Constitution forecloses any attempt to revise that judgment simply on the basis that some speech is not worth it." In other words, whether you have the right to say something doesn't depend on whether society benefits on net from you saying it.

Still, many libertarians believe part of what justifies extensive rights to free speech is that a society that respects such rights generates good consequences. For instance, John Stuart Mill argues that if you want good consequences—such as scientific progress, advancement in the arts, cultural progress, peace, and feelings of mutual respect—then you need to allow free speech *regardless* of the consequences. This may sound paradoxical. However, Mill says, the policy of only allowing beneficial speech has no history of being beneficial. The policy of allowing speech only when society judges that speech to be in its best interests has no history of being in society's best interests.

47. Are libertarians for or against capital punishment?

Libertarians generally oppose capital punishment.

Libertarians say that even if some people deserve to die, this does not mean we should empower the state to kill them. For a state to have the right to kill criminals, it must make decisions about guilt and hear appeals in a fair, competent, and reliable manner. It must have rules that reliably let the innocent—or those whose guilt is reasonably in doubt—go free.

Libertarians believe the American criminal justice system often fails to meet these standards. Perhaps a government of smart angels should be granted the right to kill certain criminals. But no realistic government has shown itself trustworthy enough to receive this license.

Why not? The philosopher Michael Cholbi (himself not a libertarian) argues that in the United States, African Americans disproportionately receive the death penalty. Statistically speaking, if white and black men with identical criminal records commit identical murders, the black man is more likely to receive the death penalty than the white man. The system is racist. Cholbi argues that we should thus have a moratorium on the death penalty.

One might object: If institutional racism is a reason to oppose the death penalty, why wouldn't it also be grounds for opposing imprisonment? The entire criminal justice system is racist. Libertarians have two responses. One response is not to regard it as an objection at all. They oppose the drug war and drug criminalization in part because they are fought in highly racist ways. (See question 50.) Libertarians' second response is if new evidence comes to light, we can let a prisoner go free. We cannot return his lost years, but we can partially compensate him and try to make amends. There is no compensating the dead.

48. Are libertarians soft on crime?

Libertarians say, if American conservatives regard them as being soft on crime, then fine, they are soft on crime, and rightly so.

More than 1 in 100 American adults is in jail. For African Americans and working-class whites, the number is about 1 in 10. Law professor Michelle Alexander says more African Americans are in prison right now than were enslaved in 1850. The United States imprisons more people than China, though China has four times the US population. Libertarians find it ironic that the so-called land of the free puts so many behind bars.

Libertarians would immediately end all "victimless" crimes, such as drug sales, gambling, and prostitution. If I want to snort coke, I should be allowed to do so. I victimize myself only in a metaphorical sense. Or, if two adults sincerely consent to exchange sex for money, they must be allowed to do so, even if the act is immoral or self-destructive. Libertarians agree that if we tolerate these activities, this will cause some lives to be destroyed. However, they say, trying to stamp out the activities not only treats adults like children but also destroys even more lives.

Libertarians want judges to have more discretion to give out lighter sentences. They want to eliminate mandatory sentences. They want to change the electoral system so that would-be district attorneys don't win elections by being "tough on crime." They would prefer to copy the better-functioning criminal justice systems found in certain European countries, such as Denmark or Sweden. Now, these countries are different from the United States, with different demographics and different poverty rates. Just because something works in Denmark does not mean it would work in the United States. Still, most other countries have far less punitive criminal justice systems and yet have less crime.

49. How would libertarians solve the problem of high crime?

Libertarians want to minimize the need for criminal justice. Most violence is born of desperation, bad circumstances, and unfortunate upbringing. To fight this, they say, we do not need more jails. At best, that's fighting fire with a squirt gun. Or perhaps that's fighting fire with gasoline. When children grow up seeing most of their neighbors going to jail, they regard criminality as normal.

The poor are disproportionately likely to commit violent crimes. The conservative response to crime is to jail the poor. Whatever good that may or may not do, it also continues the cycle of poverty and jail. The libertarian solution is to make the poor rich. Libertarians believe that instead we need to foster a society of peace and prosperity. We need to end the drug war—which itself produces more violent crime and tends to ghettoize inner cities. (See question 50.) We need to remove business licenses and regulations that prevent the poor from starting their own businesses.

Some anti-libertarians agree that ending poverty is the way to end high crime. However, they argue, the libertarian strategy for ending poverty will not succeed. Instead, they claim we need active government redistribution of wealth and antipoverty programs. A free market cannot solve poverty on its own.

50. Why do libertarians oppose the War on Drugs?

Imagine an evil demon wanted to wage war on African Americans. Imagine it wanted to turn black neighborhoods into ghettos, destroy families, increase violent crime, and impoverish their children. Imagine it also wanted to turn the police against the people, to make people live in fear of home raids. Now, because the demon is diabolical, imagine it wanted to have all this happen in the name of compassion and tough love. How might the demon do all this? Libertarians say: One good way would be to invent the American War on Drugs.

Libertarians admit that if drugs are legal, many lives will be destroyed. But, they say, because we make drugs illegal, many *more* lives are being destroyed.

In general, making drugs illegal does not make them go away. When you take something people want off the legal market, you thereby put it on the black market. From 1919 to 1933, the United States made alcohol illegal. People still drank. People couldn't buy alcohol from safe and peaceful neighborhood supermarkets, so they bought it from smugglers and violent criminals who tried to create and maintain turf empires. Prohibition made the US mafia legendary. Without alcohol prohibition, Al Capone would have been nothing more than a pimp.

What is true for alcohol is true for other drugs. Imagine illegal drugs could be sold the way alcohol is now sold. The violence associated with drug cartels and drug dealers would disappear. (We never see Coors in a shootout with Anheuser-Busch.) Street crime would go down. Gangs that depend on drug sales would fall apart.

Making drugs illegal often makes it more profitable to manufacture and sell drugs. Demand for drugs is *inelastic*.

That is, as the price of drugs increases, the quantity of drugs demanded does not decrease quite as rapidly. By making drugs illegal and thus reducing the number of suppliers, the government makes it possible to charge higher prices and make higher profits from drugs.

Nobel laureate economist Milton Friedman once joked in an interview, "The role of the government is to protect the drug cartel." The government does not *intend* to protect drug cartels, but it protects them nonetheless. In a normal market, Friedman says, there are thousands of importers. But to smuggle drugs in a black market is expensive and requires massive large-scale coordination. Only big-time cartels can afford to smuggle drugs when they are illegal. Thus, the state protects the drug cartels.

The War on Drugs reduces market competition among drug suppliers. The few remaining drug suppliers can charge monopoly prices. Again, cocaine is expensive *because* it is illegal. And because drugs are expensive, drug addicts must spend (and steal) more to feed their addiction.

Making drugs illegal also changes the kinds of drugs available. Imagine you are trying to smuggle a coca-based drug through US customs. Or, imagine you are a street dealer carrying a coca-based drug on your person. Now, suppose you can choose among three different coca-based drugs:

1. Coca leaves: large, bulky, weak potency, weak high, weakly addictive
2. Cocaine powder: less bulky, moderate potency, moderate high, moderately addictive
3. Crack cocaine: tiny bulk, strongest potency, strongest high, highly addictive

All things equal, casual drug users might prefer to chew coca leaves than to smoke crack. But dealers are worried about being caught. They thus want to carry and push the smallest, most potent, most highly addictive version of the drug. Libertarians conclude that the drug war itself selects for crack over coke and heroin over opium. You might object that users only want the strongest high. Not so. People drink beer and wine more than they drink hard liquor, and hardly anyone drinks Everclear (an extremely potent liquor).

Civil liberties columnist Glenn Greenwald says the government "destroys the lives of individuals that proponents of the drug war are trying to help. What is it we do to those we are trying to help? We take them and charge them with crimes. We turn them into felons which...renders them unemployable. We put them into cages for many years, and keep them away from their children and families." We do not do this equally, Greenwald adds. White kids are more likely to use and sell drugs than black kids, but the black kids are more likely to go to jail.

The United Nations recently estimated that in order to compromise the profitability of the drug trade, governments would need to intercept three-quarters of all imported drugs. At current levels of police power, only about 13% of heroin and about 25% of all other important drugs are confiscated. To win the War on Drugs would require a police state.

The thing is, we can get a police state even if we "lose" the War on Drugs. The United States imprisons more people for *drug* offenses than Western Europe imprisons for *all* offenses. Between 1925 and 1968, the US prison population was more or less stable at between 100,000 and 200,000 prisoners. After President Nixon declared war on drugs, the prison population grew exponentially, to over 1.6 million prisoners today. The government arrests nearly 1 million Americans yearly for marijuana possession. There are 50,000 paramilitary police raids on homes each year in the United States. (On the Internet, you can watch videos of these raids, including videos in which the police invade the wrong homes and kill innocent people.)

51. Why would libertarians legalize prostitution?

Libertarians find it bizarre that you give sex away for free but you cannot sell it. Libertarians take the view of prostitution that they take of almost everything else. If two adults consent to a transaction, and if this transaction imposes no real externality on innocent bystanders, then the transaction must be allowed. The fact that others do not like it doesn't matter.

Beyond that, libertarians think criminalizing prostitution has a similar effect on the sex trade as the War on Drugs has on drug sales. (See question 50.) Prostitution is everywhere. When we criminalize it, we make it so that prostitutes must operate in the black market. They lose police protection—and worse, they become victims of the police. Sex workers operate in dangerous environments because they operate in a black market. And, as with the War on Drugs, the War on Prostitution hurts poor minorities more than rich whites. A college-educated, upper-middle-class white woman can become a "high-class call girl" and operate in relative safety. Poor black women are more likely to have to walk the street. Finally, when prostitution is illegal, organized crime often supplies it. To criminalize prostitution is to empower the Mafia.

Some anti-libertarians dispute these empirical claims. They hold that *more* women will be exploited if prostitution were legal. Others accept the empirical claims but disagree with libertarians' moral premises. They say that prostitution so deeply violates a person's dignity that it must not be allowed. Just as a person cannot sell herself into slavery, so must she not be allowed to sell sex.

52. Why do libertarians want to allow organ sales?

Right now, about 70,000 American are on the active waitlist for kidney transplants. *Most* will not get kidneys.

Kidney sales are illegal. The legal price of a kidney is $0, far below what the market price would be if sales were legal.

When the government sets the price of a good far below the market price, this creates a shortage. Demand exceeds supply. Imagine what would happen if the government set the legal price of gasoline at $0 and said that all gasoline transfers have to be donations.

Libertarians—and many nonlibertarian bioethicists as well—argue that legalizing organ sales would reduce the kidney shortage. Organ sales would save massive numbers of lives. Few people are willing to donate their kidneys to strangers.

For example, Israel recently created a partial compensation program for living donors. Donors cannot sell organs outright, but they can now receive compensation for medical care and lost work time. This new law increased living donations by about 64% in one year. (Note that many conservative Jews oppose all organ donations, so a similar program would probably work even better in the United States.)

Almost everyone—including those who oppose legalizing organ sales—agrees that legal organ sales would save lives. However, the opposition worries that legalizing kidney sales would just allow the rich to take advantage of the poor. The poor would sell only because they are in desperate circumstances.

Still, some people complain that the poor will sell more organs than the rich. One libertarian response to this objection is to say, "Organ sales save lives *and* make the poor richer? Hooray!" Libertarians say that if we care about the poor, we must not stop them from doing what they regard as their own best option for improving their lives.

Others worry that the poor would not be educated enough to know what they are doing. Libertarians say this doesn't mean organ sales should be illegal. Instead, we could require vendors to prove they understand the costs and benefits. We could give potential vendors the information they need and make sure they understand it. We could license organ vendors the way we license drivers.

Most people find the idea of organ sales repugnant. Their stomachs turn at the thought of people selling kidneys. Some bioethicists claim there is wisdom in such repugnance. They say we should listen to our guts.

Libertarians respond: Try explaining your opposition to a little kid dying of renal failure: "Your parents are willing to pay for a kidney. Someone is willing to provide a kidney for that money. But I find the whole thing repulsive. And so I'm having the government intervene to stop the sale. Better you die than I feel disgust."

Many opponents of organ sales worry about "commodification." To commodify a thing is to make it the kind of thing that can be bought and sold on a market. Opponents say that when we commodify something, we cheapen it. We fail to signify proper respect.

Libertarians respond that even if commodifying things in some way cheapens them, there is nothing *special* about commodifying organs. The commodification worry is a worry about commodifying *anything*, not just organs. We allow people to commodify their time. A typical person sells 80,000 hours of time to employers over her life. Scientists and medical doctors commodify their expertise. We pay people to work as firefighters, police, or clergy, even though many regard these jobs as sacred callings. We allow people to sell great works of art and music. Libertarians say, if you believe commodification is repugnant, fine, be repulsed. But that's not an excuse to kill 50,000 people a year.

53. Are libertarians feminists?

Yes. Libertarians are liberal feminists. They believe all people, regardless of sex or gender identity, have the same fundamental moral status and rights. All people are entitled to the same legal standing and legal privileges.

Many libertarians agree that most countries continue to have cultural and social conditions that are oppressive to women. Most Americans explicitly affirm women's equality. They do not have explicit bias. Explicit bias is overt, self-aware sexism or racism. Explicit bias is the bias of the KKK. However, most Americans suffer from what psychologists call "implicit bias." Implicit bias occurs when a person has unconscious sexist or racist attitudes, attitudes that the person himself does not want to have.

For example, in a 1999 study, some psychologists studied *other* psychologists' implicit biases. They asked 228 male and female psychology professors to evaluate a fake teaching dossier for a hypothetical job candidate. The dossiers were identical in content, except that half were for men and half were for women. Women's dossiers received significantly lower evaluations. Or, consider that at the end of a college course, students write evaluations of their professors' teaching ability. These evaluations are used in determining rank, tenure, promotions, and raises. All students judge their professors by their looks—attractive professors get better marks than unattractive professors. However, this effect is much stronger for women. A male professor can gain a few extra pounds without much harm to his evaluations, but a slightly overweight female professor will tend to see her evaluations drop quickly.

Libertarians think governments can do little to solve these problems. Governments can help to maintain an equal legal standing and equal rights for all. But they cannot fix culture. This is a problem for civil society to solve.

Libertarianism has a reputation for being a male-dominated philosophy. Perhaps it is. However, many of the most influential libertarians were women. "Hard libertarianism" (see question 5) originated with three women: Ayn Rand, Isabel Patterson, and Rose Wilder Lane.

54. Why do libertarians support same-sex marriage?

Some of us are wired to love members of the opposite sex. Some of us are wired to love members of the same sex. Some of us are wired to find different kinds of love. Libertarians think that the state has no business judging one kind of love more worthy of honor and protection than the others.

Some libertarians believe the state should stay out of marriage entirely. Others think that the state should honor all marriage or marriage-like contracts among consenting adults.

All libertarians agree that the state must treat citizens as equals. If the state recognizes heterosexual marriage, it must recognize other forms of marriage as well.

55. Do libertarians support the right of homosexuals to adopt children?

Yes. Libertarians do not believe that homosexuality is a disqualification for being allowed to adopt children. They think gay couples have as much right to adopt as otherwise identical straight couples.

Some conservatives claim that being raised by two moms or two dads damages children. But conservatives have no evidence for this claim. On the contrary, so far, no sociologists, psychologists, or health professionals who have studied the issue have found evidence that being raised by gay parents hurts children.

56. Why do libertarians oppose the draft?

Libertarians believe that military conscription is like a kind of slavery. Under military conscription, a free person becomes— for a period of time—something much like the property of the state. Of course, the state cannot buy or sell draftees. Draftees retain many of their rights. (Note that Roman and Greek slaves had many rights, too.) But the state sends conscripted soldiers to places where others will try to kill them. It forces them to fight for causes they abhor. It forces them to kill the innocent.

Many libertarians say they can at least imagine situations in which conscription could be justified. For instance, if we faced a dire existential emergency and conscription were the only solution, then perhaps conscription may be permitted.

That said, even though we can imagine cases where conscription would be permissible, libertarians think we should forbid governments from conscripting citizens. Once governments are told, "You may conscript citizens provided it is necessary to stop a dire existential emergency," governments will see dire existential emergencies everywhere.

Libertarians also argue that volunteer armies work better than slave armies. Conscripts often do not support their cause. They have to be disciplined harder. They are less skilled and fight less effectively. In part, this is because conscripts often come from lower socioeconomic backgrounds. In part, this is because governments that may use the draft invest less in protecting and training troops. If troops die, the government can just conscript more. However, if the military has to use volunteers, it has to promise to treat them and train them better. It has to give them better weapons. Thus, libertarians think it is no surprise that the volunteer soldiers of today are more skilled, better equipped, and more effective than the conscripted soldiers in Vietnam.

President Nixon appointed libertarian economist Milton Friedman to lead a commission studying an all-volunteer military force. In one committee meeting, Friedman debated a pro-conscription general. The general said he preferred an army of conscripts because he did not want an "army of mercenaries"—that is, people who fight for money. He objected to Friedman calling an army of conscripts an "army of slaves." Friedman asked the general, "Do you really want to call people who volunteer to join the military mercenaries? If so, then you are a mercenary general. I am a mercenary professor. We are served by mercenary lawyers and doctors."

Friedman convinced Nixon to remove the draft. American men must still register for the Selective Service System. But the United States has not conscripted anyone since 1972.

Some leftist anti-libertarians want to reinstate the draft. They worry that the poor—who lack other opportunities—disproportionately volunteer for military service. (The US military denies this. It claims recruits "mirror the US population and are solidly middle class.") Some on the left believe that reinstating the draft would reduce American militarism. In an all-volunteer system, most Americans will not serve in the military. They thus favor a more interventionist or hawkish military than they otherwise would. They can externalize the cost of fighting onto volunteers. However, if going to war put them or their children at risk, they would oppose America's hawkish foreign policy.

57. Why do libertarians oppose mandatory national service?

Some conservative and even many progressive political pundits advocate compulsory national service programs. Under these programs, young adults would be required to spend two to three years in public service projects. Advocates believe mandatory service programs foster a greater sense of community, equality, and commitment to the common good. Others say these programs are needed to ensure young adults develop gratitude. Others say that mandatory service is necessary so that young adults can pay off a "debt to society."

Libertarians oppose these programs for many of the same reasons they oppose military conscription. (See question 56.)

Libertarians also say society does not do us favors the way our parents do. As a parent, out of both sincere love and a sense of duty, I invest directly in my children's welfare. In contrast, my fellow citizens do not invest in me the way my parents did. The way I benefit from society is less like how I benefited from my parents, and more like how I benefit from the sun. As the philosopher David Schmidtz says, I could not live without the sun, but it is not like the sun is doing me any favors. I am in some metaphorical sense grateful that the sun exists, but I don't owe the sun a debt.

Moreover, libertarians say, if I owe a debt to a society, it is unclear why I would specifically owe a debt to my nation-state, rather than the entire world or to my local towns or neighbor-hoods. The United States did not educate me; Hudson, New Hampshire, and Tewksbury, Massachusetts, did. I am as rich as I am because I benefited from a worldwide extended system of trade. Why think that the "society" to which I owe a debt just happens to be the United States, as opposed to Hudson, New Hampshire, or the entire world?

Libertarians say that if "kids today" aren't grateful, that doesn't mean we put a gun to their heads. We hope the world will be better off with our kids than without them. But that does not mean we should force them to be of service. I hope my young children will show gratitude when they are older. But if they leave the nest and never look back, I would not dare hire thugs to force them to "pay their debt." Just as it would be wrong for me to force my children to pay their debt, it would be wrong for society to force the youth to pay their debt.

Libertarians add: Lives other than "lives of service" serve others. Entrepreneurs, artists, businesspeople, farmers, and so on, serve society by being entrepreneurs, artists, business-people, farmers, and so on. Any decent baker does more for society by baking than by picking up litter. In people's nor-mal, daily private lives, working in a market economy, they are not merely *taking*. They are already giving back. Perhaps most people are already paying whatever debts to society they have; they just aren't paying their debts by doing "national service."

58. What do libertarians think about gun control?

Most libertarians believe we have the right to own guns.

The philosopher Michael Huemer says that by default, we should assume people have a right to own guns. The burden of proof is on those who want to restrict guns, not those who want to allow them.

Huemer argues that there is positive case for allowing guns. First, firing guns has recreational value. Many people enjoy shooting. Second, people have an extremely weighty right of self-defense. The state might be able to reduce the number of muggings, home invasions, and rapes. But, once you are being attacked, the state cannot swoop in like Superman to the rescue. At that point, you are on your own.

A study by Gary Kleck and Marc Gertz found that Americans use guns in perceived self-defense nearly 2.5 million times per year. This same study found that nearly 400,000 Americans believe gun ownership saved their lives. Of course, these Americans might be wrong—they might be exaggerating the danger they faced, and they might be mistaken in believing that a gun was necessary to save their lives. However, suppose just 1 out of 10 of these Americans were correct. Under that assumption, the number of lives saved by private gun ownership each year exceeds the number of lives lost.

Some critics object that for every intruder killed in self-defense, 43 people die from gun-related homicide or suicide or from a gun-related accident. Yet, Huemer says, this statistic is misleading. First, 37 out of those 43 deaths are suicides. Second, this objection assumes that if a gun is used successfully in self-defense, it must kill the attacker. Not so. A gun could just scare away an intruder, or better yet, make it so that the would-be burglar never intrudes in the first place.

The conservative political economist John Lott, in his controversial book *More Guns, Less Crime*, argues that allowing adults to carry concealed weapons reduces the crime rate. All things equal, states with concealed-carry laws have lower crime rates than states without such laws. Would-be rapists, intruders, and muggers worry their potential victims might be armed. Many experts disagree with Lott. However, even Lott's strongest critics tend to agree with him that, at the very least, allowing concealed weapons does not *increase* crime. They just dispute that it decreases crime.

Some libertarians oppose gun control because they want an armed citizenry to serve as a last-resort check on tyrannical government. This point of view is not unique to libertarians. For instance, the Black Panthers believed that gun control was meant to disarm blacks so the state could more easily oppress them. They believed that arming themselves helped to prevent tyranny.

59. What do libertarians think we should do about current and historical racial injustice?

There is no easy answer to this question of how we should respond to racial injustice. Libertarians disagree among themselves. Many are unsure of what to do.

Libertarians agree that everyone should be equal under the law. The state may not create classes of people with different rights and privileges.

In the past, the law made members of some ethnic groups lower status than others. Jim Crow laws, for example, required employers, retailers, and service providers to discriminate against blacks.

The effects of past racial injustice remain with us today. Some argue that to rectify this injustice, we need to redistribute wealth. Everyone agrees that this presents a problem. Most of us are innocent inheritors of a marred past. If we redistribute wealth from a rich white person to help a relatively disadvantaged African American, we would harm an innocent person to help someone who is not a direct victim.

However, the fact that redistribution would hurt innocent people is not enough to show that redistribution is wrong. Suppose your father had a Rolex, which you expected to inherit. However, suppose my father stole your father's Rolex. Suppose my father dies, and I inherit the Rolex. Suppose I did not know it was stolen. Later, you learn I have the watch and demand it back. In this case, I am innocent and you are not a direct victim. Still, in this case, justice requires me to return the Rolex. Rectification is simple in this kind of situation.

Trying to rectify past racial injustice is much more complicated. It is not clear from a moral point of view just what we should do. Some libertarians say that if certain groups are systematically disadvantaged because of past injustice, this may indeed call for some redistribution.

One misconception is that libertarians oppose all redistribution. After all, libertarians do not believe justice requires an equal distribution of wealth. (See question 78.) Thus, if whites are rich and blacks are poor, that is no problem from the libertarian point of view, or so the misconception goes. But this is a misconception.

As philosopher Matt Zwolinski says, yes, libertarians think unequal wealth can be justified. But we did not arrive at today's large inequalities of wealth by peaceful, libertarian-approved processes of voluntary exchange. Instead, he says, most land was taken by violence. Most of the wealth we currently own has a marred past. Poor people are often poor because their parents were victimized in the past. Even today, the government continues to intervene on behalf of the powerful against the weak and marginalized. In light of this historical and current injustice, we should not treat current holdings of wealth as sacrosanct from a libertarian point of view.

This does not mean that libertarians think we should confiscate all wealth, give everyone an equal share, and start over. Societies that have tried to start over from ground zero do not usually get off the ground.

Instead, we need to ask, how can we help the indirect victims of past oppression so that everyone can get beyond past injustice, and instead work together as a peaceful community of equals? Many libertarians recognize the importance of this question, but to my knowledge, few have tried to answer it.

60. Why do libertarians say that the market punishes discrimination?

Nobel laureate economist Gary Becker argues that the market tends to eliminate discrimination. Suppose people have a "taste for discrimination"—they prefer to hire whites instead of equally qualified blacks. This will tend to reduce blacks' wages. However, this gives firms willing to hire blacks an advantage. Black labor becomes a bargain. Firms can hire blacks at a lower rate, sell their products for less (because their labor costs are lower), and make higher profits.

The market *punishes* taste discrimination because it makes discrimination come at the expense of people's other selfish interests. We can imagine a society in which people would not be willing to hire or buy products from blacks under any circumstances, even to save money or to make extraordinary profits. Yet few people are really like that.

Becker's argument is not mere speculation. Economist Linda Gorman says South Africa provides a good test case. In the early 1900s, despite threats of violence and legal sanctions, white mine owners fired highly paid white workers in order to hire lower-paid blacks. The South African government created apartheid laws to stop them from hiring blacks.

Or, take Jim Crow laws. The economist Jennifer Roback says the economics of the streetcar business weighed heavily against providing separate compartments. Streetcar companies lost money and profits under Jim Crow. They had a history of actively resisting and campaigning against segregation. Southerners often accused *anti*-segregation politicians of being in streetcar companies' pockets.

Roback adds that the Southern states had a wide range of laws designed to stop blacks from competing for work. Enticement laws forbade white farm owners from trying to hire black farm workers away from other farmers during the planting or harvesting season. Black farm workers who tried to leave their jobs for higher-paying jobs could be thrown in jail. Vagrancy laws required blacks to be employed at all times. Any unemployed black man was considered a vagrant and could be put on a chain gang. Thus, blacks could not search for better employment; they had to stick with whatever job they had. Emigrant-agent laws forbade white recruiters from enticing laborers to leave their current cities or states to take jobs elsewhere. These and other laws and regulations were created to stop the market from helping blacks.

Jim Crow was expensive. Train companies lost money by having to run extra train cars. Lunch counters lost money by having to supply twice as many bathrooms.

Southern states *required* private companies to mistreat blacks. The laws were there because many businesses did not discriminate until forced to do so. If you read old newspaper editorials from the Southern states under Jim Crow, you'll frequently find editors complaining that greedy businessmen just chase the dollar and are unwilling to uphold the moral ideal of segregation.

61. Would libertarians allow private business discrimination?

Libertarians think that business owners have at least a *prima facie* right to hire whomever they please for whatever reason they please. If a Korean grocer just wants to hire other Koreans, then she should be free to do so.

The government does not forbid you from discriminating against people in your private life. No one thinks it should be illegal for a white woman only to date white men, even if there are better-qualified black men available. You can decide only to befriend members of your own ethnic group, if you so choose. Such discrimination is stupid and immoral, but that does not mean the government should stop you.

Libertarians think that, at least by default, businesses should also be allowed this kind of stupid and immoral discrimination. Libertarians think that a genuinely free market *punishes* discrimination (see question 60), and so a market will tend to correct the problem over time.

However, many libertarians say there are limits in principle to the right to discriminate against minority job applicants or customers. It's one thing if we face discrimination here or there from time to time. However, suppose discrimination becomes extremely pervasive. Many libertarians believe that property rights—including the right to run our businesses as we see fit—can be justified only if they systematically benefit everyone who is asked to respect those rights. If property rights end up systematically leaving some people behind, it may be unreasonable to demand that those left behind respect those property rights. Some libertarians argue that in these cases, in order to preserve the legitimacy of the system of property rights as a whole, we may be required to forbid private business discrimination.

6

ECONOMIC FREEDOM

62. What economic rights do libertarians believe we have?

We have a general right to conduct our financial and commercial affairs as we see fit, without having to justify ourselves or answer to society at large. Just as recognizing religious liberty requires the general protection of independent activity in the religious realm, economic liberty requires the general protection of independent activity in economic matters.

Libertarians claim that, as a matter of basic justice, people have the right to acquire, hold, use, give, and in many cases destroy personal property. They may decide what to eat, drink, and wear and determine what kinds of entertainment and cultural experiences they will consume. They may acquire wealth for themselves or for others. They have the right to enter into a wide range of contracts for the exchange of goods and services. They may enter into and negotiate employment contracts (including wage rates, hours worked, working conditions, and so on) as they see fit. They may decide for themselves how to balance leisure and work. They may choose to join unions or not. They may manage their households as they see fit. They may create things for sale. They have the right to start, manage, and stop businesses; to sell franchises in such businesses; and to run such businesses for their own private ends in the way they regard as best. This includes the right to form certain kinds of joint ventures, including certain kinds of corporations and workers' cooperatives. People may own private productive property, such as factories or machinery, and develop property for productive purposes. They may acquire, lend, take risks with, and profit from capital and financial instruments. They have the right to determine their own long-term financial plans, including retirement saving and investments in certain forms of insurance. Libertarians even believe that people have the right to sell sexual services or their own body parts, such as kidneys.

Libertarians believe economic liberty is a fundamental or basic human right, morally on par with the rights of free speech or freedom of conscience. Libertarians believe that each person has a robust and extensive set of economic liberties.

Some anti-libertarians believe that if people have such extensive economic rights, then a large percentage of people will end up living poor and miserable lives. These anti-libertarians believe that markets create winners and losers. They believe that to ensure that the worst off lead decent lives, we must greatly constrain the scope of economic liberty.

63. Are libertarians only concerned about economic issues?

No. Libertarians advocate giving everyone increased sovereignty over all aspects of their lives. Yet when they protest wars or fight in favor of gay marriage, they blend in with others. When libertarians defend markets, they stand out. This may create the misimpression that libertarians only care about economic liberty.

64. Why do libertarians think economic freedom is important?

Libertarians believe economic freedom is necessary if people are to be authors of their own lives. If we are to respect people as self-authors—as people who have the right to write their own stories—we need to afford them wide latitude to choose for themselves. The neoclassical liberal philosopher John Tomasi argues, "Restrictions of economic liberty, no matter how lofty the social goal, impose conformity on the life stories that free citizens might otherwise compose" for themselves.

Libertarians think we need economic freedom to respect human diversity. We are not all the same. There's no one way of life that's best for all. Economic freedom empowers each person to pursue her own conception of the good life.

In life, we face difficult questions: How should I make trade-offs between work and leisure? What career should I pursue? Should I take a loan? Should I run a business? Should I invest? Under what terms? What makes for a meaningful life for me? These questions are deeply personal. Libertarians say we must not treat people like children. We must not subjugate them and answer these questions for them. Instead, we must give everyone wide latitude to decide for themselves. The economic liberties and of property rights empower people to act upon their own conceptions of the good life.

Left-liberals agree with libertarians that the civil liberties are important. Yet they do not see why most economic liberties could matter for a person's sense of self. Some left-liberals want to protect citizens from economic decisions, much as I protect my four-year-old. Libertarians want to empower people to make these decisions for themselves.

Libertarians say that controlling one's own economic decisions is part of what it means to be the author of one's own life. Tomasi asks us to put ourselves in the shoes of Amy, owner of Amy's Pup-in-the-Tub in Warren, Rhode Island. Tomasi says to the left-liberal: You understand why an artist can find meaning in life when she finishes a painting. You understand why a philosopher can find meaning when she writes a treatise. If so, then you should also understand what it means for Amy to run a business by her own entrepreneurial vision.

Libertarians believe freedom of commerce under the rule of law empowers people to cooperate on a massive scale, liberating each other from poverty. Ten thousand years ago, everyone everywhere was poor. For most of history, most people lived on less than a dollar per day, on what the UN would describe as extreme poverty. The average person is about 30 times richer now than in 1800. Measuring GDP in constant dollars, the United States today has an economic output that is about 50% greater than the entire world's output in 1950.

We did not become rich by adjusting marginal tax rates. We became wealthy by unleashing human ingenuity. What happened? Economist Deirdre McCloskey says: Once we were all poor. Then capitalism happened, and now, as a result, we're rich. Libertarians say: Even Marxists have to be thankful for markets in some sense. As a matter of fact, the working class enjoys prosperity and positive liberty in market economies, but almost nowhere else.

Libertarians argue that if we want people to be secure, certain economic decisions must not be left to democratic deliberation or bargaining. For instance, imagine everyone got to deliberate and vote on what career *you* should pursue. You would feel oppressed, not empowered. Democratic decision making does not imbue people with control over their own lives; it strips them of it. When you vote with others as an equal, your vote makes no difference. Libertarians thus want to insulate people from political bargaining. Economic liberty and private property means they ask others' permission to lead their own lives as they see fit.

65. Why do libertarians believe property rights in particular are important?

Property rights are useful the way traffic lights are useful. At a crowded intersection, we need to know who goes first. We solve that problem by saying whoever has a green light gets to go. That might seem unjust. After all, the person with the red light might be more deserving or needy. However, imagine if every time we came to an intersection, we had to stop, rank everyone by need, and then let the neediest go first. The system would distribute right of way according to need, and yet it would almost never actually help the needy.

Without property rights, the question of who gets to use what becomes a constant political battle. Society is a kind of traffic. Property rights make that traffic run smoothly.

Property rights solve problems. We can see what problems they solve by examining what happens without them.

Imagine that some resource is left in the "commons." Everyone is free to use it, but no one owns it. For example, suppose 10 shepherds, each of whom has 10 sheep, use a common pasture. Let's say the sheep are worth $100 each on the market. The total economic output of the land is $10,000 per year.

Suppose the pasture can sustain 100 sheep indefinitely, but if there are 101 or more sheep, the pastures starts to die and turn to dust. Now suppose a shepherd experiments with adding an 11th sheep to his flock. There now isn't enough grass to feed all the sheep. Each individual sheep is worth $95 instead of $100. Yet, for the shepherd who added an 11th sheep to his flock, this is still a good deal. His flock of 11 sheep is now worth $1,045 instead of $1,000.

However, think of the other shepherds. Their flocks are now worth only $950 instead of $1,000. They will probably try to recover their losses by adding sheep, too. And so, the pasture is doomed.

The ecologist Garrett Hardin dubs this phenomenon the "tragedy of the commons." When no one owns a resource, people have little incentive to maintain it. Worse, they have an incentive to extract as much value as they can from it before others do. So, it's no surprise that fishermen are destroying ocean stocks.

Or, consider that certain societies have experimented with the following rule: Whenever anyone bakes a pie, hunts a deer, or grows some beans, everyone is entitled to an equal share. Many societies that experiment with this rule—such as the Jamestown colony or early Mormon settlements—starve and then abandon it. In practice, when people live by that rule, few people work. No one wants to bake a pie when he gets only one bite and his neighbors get the rest. In practice, "everyone gets an equal share" is often equivalent to "everyone gets no share."

66. How do libertarians respond to the Marxist worry that property rights are "merely formal"?

A penniless beggar has the right to buy bread, but that won't feed him. Marxists say legal property rights are "merely formal." Marxists conclude formal property rights are worthless without guarantees of wealth.

A libertarian might respond that from the armchair, the Marxist worry sounds right. But, libertarians respond, what if we treated it as a testable empirical claim? What happens when "merely formal" property rights are secure, and what happens when they are not?

The economist Hernando de Soto says that in the West, we find pockets of poverty. In the rest of the world, we find pockets of wealth. What explains the difference? De Soto says that the poorest of the world's poor possess roughly $10 trillion worth of land. Yet they do not own this land the way westerners do. In countries like Peru or Egypt, most people lack formal legal titles to their land. Most people do not have or work in legally recognized businesses.

De Soto researched what it would take for the poor to acquire property rights in their land or to acquire legal recognition of their businesses. In Egypt, for instance, he found the process would take six hours a day for a year, and cost more (in fees and bribes) than the average annual income.

De Soto argues that the lack of formal property rights is one of the main reasons the world's poor stay poor. A westerner can mortgage his land to start a business. His counterpart in Peru cannot take his land to the bank. A westerner can trade with anyone around the world, secure in his ability to recover damages if someone breaks a contract. His counterpart in rural Peru can only trade with people he knows personally. The person who would start a chain of Peruvian restaurants in northern Virginia runs a food cart in Lima. The food cart operator has no police protection for his business and no recourse to courts to settle disputes. He lacks the legal means to sell franchises or to post share offerings on a stock exchange; indeed, he cannot even raise capital for a proper building with a proper kitchen.

De Soto concludes that Marxists are half right and half wrong. Formal property rights are not a panacea, but without them the world's poor have little hope of raising themselves out of poverty. Formal property rights do not guarantee prosperity for all, but, then, nothing does. However, there is no history of people being prosperous without such rights.

67. Do libertarians think property rights are absolute?

Rights impose duties. For instance, my right to life imposes a duty on others not to kill me.

Sometimes moral duties can be overridden by other factors. For instance, if I promise to meet you for dinner at 6 p.m., then I should be there on time. Yet, suppose I find a helpless lost child on the way to dinner. My obligation to help the child can override my duty to meet you on time.

Absolute rights, by definition, cannot be overridden. Thus, suppose my property rights were absolute. Now imagine you are walking in the street by my house. Suddenly a drunk driver swerves toward you. Suppose you can dodge out of the car's way only by jumping onto my land, without my permission. If property rights were absolute, it would be wrong for you to dodge the car.

Most libertarians deny property rights are absolute. Most accept that in the aforementioned example, you may jump on my lawn without my permission.

Libertarians believe that property rights, like other rights, are weighty, but not absolute. Rights can be overridden, but not for just any reason. You can trespass on my land to dodge a car, but you can't have a picnic there whenever you please.

Libertarians argue that we should not override property rights just because overriding them here or there would be more useful or efficient in single instances. If people can't count on their property rights, they can't make stable long-term plans. If people know their property rights can be overridden whenever society deems it useful to do so, they then cannot trust the property system anymore. (Similarly, try to imagine a world in which individual promises could be broken whenever doing so would be slightly more useful than not. In that world, there would be little trust.)

Also, libertarians say, to serve the common good, be careful empowering governments to override property rights in the name of the common good. When given such power, governments may pay lip service to the common good and then use the power mostly to serve the privileged elite. For instance, in the United States, governments use the power of eminent domain to kick the poor out of their homes to make way for big box stores and sports team owners.

Some critics of libertarianism respond that while the government does sometimes abuse eminent domain to help the wealthy, it usually uses it to provide needed infrastructure or public housing.

68. Why are libertarians so concerned about economic growth, prosperity, and wealth?

The Marxist philosopher G. A. Cohen once argued that money is like a ticket. The more money you have, the more tickets you have to do things.

Wealth thus tends to increase positive liberty. (See question 14.) Positive liberty is the power to achieve one's ends. For instance, when we say a bird is free to fly, we mean that the bird has the power to fly.

For most of us, increased wealth means the increased power, capacity, or ability to do as we please. Wealth liberates. Wealth enables us to lead more authentic lives. Wealth makes us better able to pursue and realize our conceptions of the good life. For instance, had I been born into a poorer America a century ago, I would not have been able to pursue my dream of becoming an academic. I would have worked instead in a textile factory.

Wealth also tends to make us happier. Economists Betsy Stevenson and Justin Wolfers have shown that people's happiness and satisfaction strongly correlate with their absolute levels of wealth. (Stevenson's and Wolfers's data come from the 2006 Gallup World Poll, which surveyed 130,000 people from 100 countries.) As Nobel laureate psychologist Daniel Kahneman summarizes, "Humans everywhere, from Norway to Sierra Leone,... evaluate their life by a common standard of material prosperity, which changes as GDP increases."

Libertarians think we need economic growth to maintain a "positive-sum society." In a positive-sum society, everyone can become better off at the same time. A stationary or no-growth economy is a zero-sum society. In a zero-sum society, you can become better off only if others simultaneously fall. When there is no economic growth, for you to get an extra $10,000 to pursue your own projects, others have to lose $10,000. Libertarians advocate a society in which others' talents are a boon to us, not a threat. Yet without economic growth, we tend to look upon each other with envy and suspicion.

69. Why do libertarians support markets?

Liberal market societies do not offer guarantees. But, libertarians say, market societies offer something better: results. Critics of market society say the formal freedom that liberal society guarantees is not enough. Real freedom, they say, is a matter of what workers can *do*, not what others can't do to them. Libertarians respond that this real freedom is found in market society and almost nowhere else.

Libertarians believe a free market means free people. To say a market is unfree is to say someone stops other people from making voluntary, mutually advantageous trades.

Commerce is implicitly an egalitarian idea. In commerce, no one commands and no one obeys. A tyrant can force subordinates to follow his commands. But under normal conditions, a shoemaker cannot force any customers to trade with him. To profit in a free market, one must induce others to trade voluntarily. No one is obligated to accept the terms of trade. The legitimacy of a transaction depends on whether everyone consents.

This means, as Adam Smith realized, that for me to benefit from market exchange, I must benefit others. To get bread from a baker, I must give something he wants in exchange. This desire for profit keeps the market in alignment and coordinates everyone's activities.

Markets push agents to anticipate the results of their choices. Markets reward people who create value for others with profits. They punish people who destroy value for others with losses.

Markets decentralize decision making, giving each agent the power to buy and sell without having to ask permission. They thus enable individuals to cooperate with one another on a massive scale without having to debate or settle on questions of value. Markets enable people to experiment—to practice and try out different alternatives. Markets also provide a large range of alternatives. We can create our own niches and live as we please, by our own conceptions of the good life, provided we respect others' ability to do the same.

70. Why do libertarians support free trade between countries?

Economists have long said there is usually no stronger of an argument to restrict trade between countries as there is to restrict trade between individual cities or between individual people within the same country. Trade is trade. It makes as much sense to protect America from China as to protect New York City from Newark.

Should the government use quotas or tariffs to make us buy domestic goods? Libertarians respond that one reliable, if imperfect, test that something is a positive-sum game, or at least not a negative-sum game, is this: If given a choice, do people want to play it? If we have to chain people to the bargaining table to keep them from walking away, then we have to suspect we're not playing a game everyone can win.

Many people assume free trade helps the rich at the expense of the poor. In contrast, libertarians think protectionism protects the well connected, not the poor. When Adam Smith wrote *The Wealth of Nations*, England had tariffs and restrictions on linen imports. Lawmakers claimed these tariffs benefited everyone. However, Smith found, only the final weaved products fetched much profit. The poorest workers—female spinners who produced the basic threads—made nothing off of the tariffs. The tariffs limited their market and kept the price of the yarn low. This helped factory owners, not poor spinners. Also, by restraining trade, clothing manufacturers kept the overall price of clothing higher. Smith asked: When linen prices are high, whom does this hurt the most, the silk-wearing rich who own clothing factories, the professional middle class with disposable income, or the poor?

Smith observes that specialization is one of the main secrets of prosperity. When individuals specialize, they become more productive. They can trade with one another, allowing everyone to become richer than if they had tried to be self-sufficient.

The size of the market determines the degree of specialization. On an isolated farm, a farmer's family has to do just about everything that needs doing. They can buy their tools in the village perhaps, but they do the rest themselves. In a village, a person can make a living as a carpenter, repairing a farmer's axles, wheels, wagon bed, or roof; carving a yoke for oxen; and doing just about anything a farmer needs that requires woodworking skills. In a city servicing a national market, a carpenter can specialize in manufacturing ax handles, or violins. In a commercial port serving a global market, a company can hire a staff of carpenters.

The goal of being self-sufficient often leads to war. Imagine you decide to be self-sufficient. You refuse to buy from others. Now suppose you need oil (or anything else your little plot of land doesn't supply). If you don't have oil under your lawn, and if you refuse to buy it from others, then your only option is to seize it through force. And so, throughout history, when nations decide to become "self-sufficient," they always build empires. If goods cannot cross national borders through trade, then they must be incorporated into one's borders through war.

When we trade with others, we are not self-sufficient in the sense of creating everything we need for ourselves. We do very much depend upon others. However, Smith thought, interdependence is not dangerous. David Schmidtz summarizes: In Smith's view, on a free market, we are "dependent on many, [but] at the mercy of nobody."

71. Are libertarians just trying to protect the interests of big business?

What does it mean to be pro-business? We often think of pro-business politicians as giving out subsidies, privileges, and special contracts to large corporations, taxing the poor to give to the rich. Libertarians oppose all such activities. Adam Smith and the other classical liberals were the first and still are the most consistent defenders of the view that government should not support business. For them, being in favor of the market means letting it be rather than trying to prop up industry through government handouts. For them, being in favor of markets means letting markets punish corporations for bad decisions. If GM can survive only with government handouts, libertarians say let it die.

Many critics believe libertarians are "in the pocket" of big business. Libertarianism sells itself as a philosophy of freedom. But, critics say, in practice, libertarian freedom is just freedom for corporations with servitude and poverty for everyone else.

Critics claim that libertarian policies would benefit the powerful corporations at the expense of everyone else. Libertarianism would guarantee that an elite few capture most wealth, while the common person is left behind. Libertarianism, the critics say, is a recipe for brewing robber barons.

Critics expect libertarians to respond by saying, "If economic freedom leads to monopoly, corporate dominance, and poverty for the masses, so be it. That's the price of freedom." This is not libertarians' response.

Libertarians respond to their progressive critics, "Runaway corporatism is *your* fault. You may claim to oppose big business and crony capitalism. However, when in power, whether intentionally or not, you support big business at the expense of the common person."

Progressive politics enables the government to choose winners and losers in the economy. When a government is empowered to choose winners and losers, the well-connected will be the winners.

Libertarians claim that through the Democratic Party, the moderate Left has held significant power in the United States for 80 years. Democrats empowered the federal government to regulate the economy in order to control and restrain corporate power. However, libertarians claim, corporations and the financial elite have captured that very power for their own advantage.

Imagine you lived in a bizarre, magical world, in which every time you tried to increase the power of the police to fight violent crime, violent criminals magically seized that very power and became even more violent. In that kind of world, you would not want to give the police more power. In that world, if you spent 80 years giving the police more power, you would in turn be to blame for crime. Libertarians say that when it comes to regulating corporate power, we live in precisely this bizarre, magical world.

However, it is not magic. Rather, the mechanisms that explain the rise of corporatism and crony capitalism are well understood. One just needs to study a branch of economics called *public choice economics*. Public choice economics, developed by Nobel laureates James Buchanan and Kenneth Arrow, as well as Gordon Tullock, Anthony Downs, and Mancur Olson, applies the insights of microeconomics to understand and explain political behavior.

Both libertarians and most of the Left oppose corporatism and crony capitalism. The Left says, "Corporations have too much power. Let's increase government power over corporations." Libertarians say, "Corporations have too much power. Let's decrease government power over corporations." Libertarians admit that their solution, on its face, looks absurd. However, they claim that when we increase government power over corporations, corporations in turn capture that power to benefit themselves. To increase government power over corporations is to increase corporate power.

Libertarians say: Are corporations too powerful? The power to regulate the economy is the same thing as the power to distribute favors. When we create government agencies with the power to control the rules of the economic game, corporations will compete to lobby for, purchase, and control that very power. The more unscrupulous the corporation and the more it has at stake in controlling the agency, the more it will spend to get control. It is no accident that there is a set of revolving doors among the Obama administration and Goldman Sachs. (For example, Obama's chief of staff for the US Treasury is a former Goldman Sachs lobbyist. The deputy director of the NEC is a former Goldman Sachs analyst. Obama's undersecretary of state of economic, business, and agricultural affairs was a former vice president at Goldman Sachs. Incidentally, Goldman Sachs was Obama's second-largest campaign donor in 2008.)

Consider: Why does American Coca-Cola have corn syrup when Mexican Coca-Cola has sugar? The reason: The corn lobby is powerful in the United States. The US government subsidizes corn and other cereals, feeding nearly $3 billion to large agribusinesses such as Archer Daniels Midland. The Energy Policy Act of 2005 guarantees a market for corn by requiring (corn-based) ethanol to be added to gasoline. The United States also imposes a tariff-rate quota on foreign-produced sugar. Libertarians note that subsidies favor big business. The government distributes farm subsidies on the basis of crop and crop size. Factory farms get larger subsidies than family farms.

The United States does not have, and has never had, a free market. Instead, it has always had a market in which Congress and the White House can pick favorites at the expense of everyone else. The nineteenth century was no economic libertarian utopia. Instead, the United States imposed heavy tariffs on foreign goods in order to protect domestic corporate interests. Railroad companies enjoyed heavy subsidies, special privileges in the seizure of land, and monopoly protection. (By the early twentieth century, nearly every transcontinental railroad subsidized by the US government went bankrupt, while the only unsubsidized railroad prospered.)

The progressive Left often complains that corporations are too big. However, libertarians say, the Left's favored policies distort the market in favor of larger and larger corporations. The more we regulate the economy, the bigger big business will tend to be. Complying with regulations costs money and time. The larger your company is, the more easily you can keep up with the rules. The US Small Business Administration (SBA)—a government agency—reports that complying with all regulations costs firms on average $10,585. However, these costs are not evenly dispersed. The SBA claims that small businesses face about 36% higher costs than large businesses. Previous studies have estimated that it costs small firms 60% more than large firms to comply with federal regulations. Or, consider that when governments require employers to provide health care and other benefits, this is much more costly to small firms than large corporations. Or, consider why drug companies have to be big. With current FDA regulations in place, it takes on average 12 years and a billion dollars to bring a drug to market in the United States. How could anything other than a huge pharmaceutical company survive in this environment? Complicated tax codes, regulatory regimes, and licensing rules naturally select for larger corporations. Regulations, tax codes, and licensing rules are like a regressive tax that disadvantages the small.

The progressive Left often complains that financial firms and large banks take too much financial risk. The Left believes this is because managers are irrational and greedy. Libertarians say that no doubt, some are. Still, part of the story has to be that the government incentivizes what would otherwise be irrational behavior. The Clinton administration wanted to increase home ownership in the United States. The government-sponsored enterprises (GSEs) Fannie Mae and Freddie Mac were instructed to buy ever more risky mortgages from banks. To comply with the Community Reinvestment Act, the GSEs and banks had to provide loans to lower-income borrowers with lower down-payment and capital requirements. Banks had strong incentives to write loans to risky clients, knowing they could then sell these loans to the GSEs. Finally, the government has in the past repeatedly bailed out large corporations. This means that corporations expect bailouts and act accordingly. As left-leaning economist John Galbraith says, "Roughly speaking, if you are in trouble and big enough, you will be rescued and recapitalized in one way or another by the government." If the US government commits to bailing out Wells Fargo, then the market responds by creating more Wells Fargos. As long as a corporation is large enough and well connected, it can socialize risk but privatize profits. We encourage banks to be large and to take more risks.

The progressive Left complains that large corporations bully private persons and small firms. However, a principal way corporations bully others is by getting local governments to seize property on their behalf. The governmental power of eminent domain allows governments to take private property (after compensating owners) for public use. The purpose of this power originally was to allow governments to build needed public structures and provide public goods. However, in *Kelo v. City of New London* (2005), the US Supreme Court decided that seizing property for the purpose of economic development constituted public use. If a private developer can convince your local government that it can help the local economy, the developer may ask your government to take your property, shut down your store, or destroy your farm. The libertarian legal advocacy group the Institute for Justice tried to stop the *Kelo* decision and frequently provides pro bono services to the poor to help stop eminent domain abuse.

Libertarians think it is no anomaly that the Obama administration fed millions of taxpayer dollars to Solyndra. It is no accident that Amazon is now lobbying in favor of an Internet sales tax (which would disadvantage its competitor eBay). Released documents indicate that the now-defunct Enron lobbied for cap-and-trade regulations because they would hurt their competitors. Libertarians say all of this is to be expected. The US government has significant legal power over corporate America. Corporate America uses its influence and money to control that very power for its own interests.

Public choice economists call this phenomenon "rent seeking." "Rent seeking" refers to nonvoting, noncriminal activities that individuals or firms engage in with the purpose of either changing the laws or regulations or changing how the laws and regulations are administered, for the purpose of securing a benefit. A firm engages in rent seeking when it seeks to gain an economic privilege or advantage from governmental manipulation of the market environment. James Buchanan says, "If the government is empowered to grant monopoly rights or tariff protection to one group, at the expense of the general public or of designated losers, it follows that potential beneficiaries will compete for the prize."

Libertarianism offers a solution for corporate rent seeking. Crony capitalism and corporatism are like runaway fires. Progressives want to increase government power over the market, but libertarians believe this is just throwing fuel on the fire. Libertarians want to kill the fire by removing the fuel. When governments can pick winners and losers in the economy, big business always wins. Libertarians say that if we minimize government regulatory power over the economy, then corporations will have no power to compete for, no rents to seek, no subsidies to enjoy, and no agencies to capture. They will be able to beat competitors only through open market competition, that is, by producing what consumers believe is the best overall package of products and services.

On this point, a libertarian might note that, according to Transparency International, New Zealand, Denmark, Switzerland, Australia, Hong Kong, and Canada each have less corrupt governments than the United States. At the same time, the conservative Heritage Foundation ranks the economies of these countries as freer than or at least as free as the United States. (Denmark scores very slightly lower because of its high tax rates. However, Denmark also rates 99.1 in business freedom, 90.0 in investment freedom, and 90.0 in financial freedom. In comparison, the United States scores 91.1, 70.0, and 70.0, respectively, on these measures.) Freedom from corruption and economic freedom are strongly correlated.

72. Why do libertarians believe socialism causes the worst to get on top?

In the twentieth century, Marxist governments were *deadlier* than the two world wars. In *The Black Book of Communism*, Stéphane Courtois and his coauthors document how in the twentieth century, *outside of war*, communist governments killed between 80 and 100 million of their own citizens. The rise of communist governments was one of the worst humanitarian disasters, ever.

Libertarians don't view command-economy socialism as a way of freeing or empowering the poor. They view it as a way of helping the powerful run and destroy other people's lives. That may not be how socialists advertise themselves. But, libertarians say, there hasn't been an exception to that rule, yet.

Central planning requires a great concentration of great power. For a government to plan an economy, it needs to control almost everything. (Note that this spills over into how we can exercise our civil liberties. Want to publish a newspaper? That takes resources that the central planners control.)

When people compete for this power, bad people have an advantage. Someone like Stalin will do whatever it takes to get power, free of moral constraint.

Economist F. A. Hayek asks, why have Marxist revolutionary socialists succeeded in creating socialist states, while democratic socialists have never held power long enough to implement their plans? (Or, more precisely, when the democratic socialists do hold power, why do they fail to implement real socialism?) The democratic socialist's own values—such as liberality, rights, and respect for individuals—inhibit them from doing what it takes to make plans work. Revolutionary Marxists impose harsh discipline on themselves and others. They don't value individual life. They are willing to kill whoever stands in their way.

Central plans must be administered coercively. If you try to plan an entire economy all at once, you can't let people make their own plans, as capitalist societies do. You need everyone to do her part. You can try using carrots, but carrots leave people a choice. You'll have to resort to sticks instead.

Intellectuals do not make good central planners. Intellectuals are not single-minded. They challenge ideas. They disagree. Instead, central planners need to be those who tow the party line.

Liberal, democratic assemblies do not make good central planners. Liberal democratic assemblies may want to promote the common good. But, being democratic, they won't agree on just what that means or how to do it. They will disagree. They will make slow decisions. They'll get mired in gridlock and will end up having to choose one person to have dictatorial power.

Hayek adds that central planning requires that people regard the plans as their own. So, it requires propaganda. For those who can't be controlled by propaganda, it requires something like a KGB. You'll need to spy on people to see who goes along with the plan and who doesn't.

73. Why do libertarians believe socialism fails to create prosperity?

Libertarians have no problem with communal property. For instance, most spouses share property. If people voluntarily wish to share property among an entire community, they should be free to do so. People have the right to form Kibbutzes or other communes. Libertarians just say that no one should be conscripted into these communities.

There is a difference between voluntary socialist coopera-tives and large-scale socialist economies. Libertarians claim that state socialism cannot work on any large scale.

An extended economy requires that millions (and nowa-days, billions) of people can coordinate their activities to produce a good outcome. It requires that people have the information to know what is best for them to do and also have the incentive to do it.

Markets coordinate billions of people without anyone doing the coordinating. Compare markets to the military. Armies have strict hierarchies. The commander-in-chief sets a goal. Generals plot strategies and deliver orders to lesser officers below them. In turn, orders spread, with increasing levels of specificity, down to the lowest private. Privates follow orders; they do not set their own goals. In contrast, in a free market, no one is a general. (Alternatively, we could say that everyone is a general. In markets, everyone is a planner or a strategist to some degree.) So how do markets hold together? How can there be order if no one is giving orders?

Following Nobel laureate economist F. A. Hayek, libertarians claim that a functioning economy needs three things:

1. *Information*: Something must signal to individuals what they need to do.
2. *Incentives*: Something must induce people to act on that information.
3. *Learning*: Something must correct people's mistakes and teach people to become better at responding to information and incentives.

Market economies serve these needs with three mechanisms:

1. *Information:* Prices
2. *Incentives:* Private property
3. *Learning:* Profits and losses

Libertarians say that it is possible to run an economy with prices, private property, and profits and losses. Certain small communities can get by without them. But large-scale economies cannot.

In a command economy, only a few people plan. In a market, everyone plans. When it comes to economic planning, 7 billion heads are usually better than one. Each person on the market has different information about the economy, about local opportunities and costs, and especially about her own wants and desires. For an economic system to function, this diffuse information must be conveyed to the planners. When economists say that prices are a function of supply and demand, they're saying that prices convey this diffuse information to the planners. In markets, prices are measurements.

When command economies set prices, prices don't measure anything. Artificial, government-mandated prices convey no information about scarcity or demand. Without real prices, planners cannot perform reliable economic calculations.

Without a price system, they can't reliably decide whether producing apples or oranges is more productive. How would central planners know whether to use plastic or metal shovels, gold or aluminum wire, or leather or canvas in shoes? (It requires that one hold in mind a precise inventory of the quantities and qualities of all the different factors of production in the entire system, together with full geographic knowledge and possibilities open to different locations, all at once, and be able to go through all the possible permutations.) The simple answer is they don't know, so they guess. And, so, they remain poor.

74. Why do libertarians tend to oppose government interventions into the economy?

Economists say government intervention can be justified, in principle, in order to correct market failures. Libertarians agree that markets can and do fail. However, libertarians think that market failures must be balanced against *government failures.* When governments are given the power to regulate markets or fix market failures, they often make things worse, not better. Libertarians think that once we account for government failure, we have much less reason to favor government interventions into the economy. (For a fuller account of this point, see question 36.)

Libertarians say that such government interventionism leads to crony capitalism and corporatism. Libertarians believe the progressive Left has caused corporate power to get out of control. (For more on this, see question 71.)

Hardly anyone now supports command economy socialism. Most recognize that central planning fails. Most recognize that central planning is inefficient and fails to produce prosperity. Most people recognize that planning an entire economy is impossible. (See questions 72 and 73.)

However, libertarians claim people do not recognize a related point. *Planning* a huge economy is impossible; economies are

too complex. *Managing* and *controlling* a market-based economy are thus extremely difficult, if not impossible.

Those who wish to regulate, manage, and control the economy regard it as a kind of machine. They view bureaucrats
and central bankers as engineers and mechanics who keep the
economic engine running smoothly.

Libertarians say that a market economy is not a machine.
Rather, the market is an ecosystem. The Federal Reserve, politicians, and regulators are less like engineers tweaking an
engine and more like park rangers trying to control a jungle.
Just like a jungle, a market has a logic of its own. For instance,
a regulator can dictate that it is illegal to hire an unskilled
laborer at less than $20 per hour. But a regulator cannot dictate
that people will actually want to hire unskilled laborers at $20
per hour.

Markets are *harder* to manage than jungles. Jungles have an
internal logic and react in unforeseen ways when we attempt
to control them. Still, a jungle just does what a jungle does.
Markets, on the other hand, are populated by real people with
plans of their own. Actors in markets play *strategically.* When
regulators attempt to control them or influence them, market
actors work to counteract or take advantage of the control and
influence.

On this point, consider the work of economists Thomas
Sargent and Christopher Sims, joint winners of the 2011 Nobel
Prize in economics, and of Robert Lucas, winner of the 1995
Nobel Prize. Sargent, Lucas, and Sims developed a "rational
expectations" theory in macroeconomics. Rational expectations theory says that, as a whole, market agents are not
systematically wrong in their prediction of the future of the
market. They make mistakes, but these mistakes tend to be
random and to cancel each other out. (Note: Rational expectations theory allows for asset bubbles to occur.)

To the extent rational expectations theory is correct, many
government interventions are doomed to fail. For instance,
macroeconomics textbooks used to recommend that central

banks inflate the currency whenever there is high employment. The hope was that central banks could drive up prices by pumping newly printed bills into the economy. This would then "trick" employers into believing that effective demand for their products is higher than it really is. The duped employers would then want to hire more workers. Workers would accept normal wages, because wages tend to rise more slowly in response to inflation than many other prices. High unemployment would thus end. At least, that was the hope.

This kind of intervention works only if the central bank can trick employers and workers. Rational expectations theory says the bank cannot trick them. Rational expectations theory says we cannot predict ahead of time what employers or workers will think the real rate of inflation will be. Instead, rational expectations theory says that when the Federal Reserve inflates the supply of money, market agents tend to realize it's doing so. Market agents adjust their demand for currency accordingly. Employers do not want to hire more workers—as a whole, they know the Fed created the high prices. Employees want higher wages—as a whole, they know the Fed made prices go up. This means that the Fed cannot cure unemployment by printing dollar bills.

Finally, libertarians say, government interventions lead to more interventions. When governments intervene, regardless of the good they do, they also tend to produce unforeseen bad consequences. They then tend to intervene again to correct those unforeseen bad consequences. For instance, when cities set rent controls, this tends to cause a shortage of housing for the poor. This in turn pushes the city to have to build public housing. Or, libertarians say, US housing policy induced banks to take bad risks. (See question 92.) This led to a financial crisis, and that in turn pressured the government to have to pass an expensive economic recovery bill.

Some anti-libertarians say that libertarians are right that government interventions often fail. However, they claim, such interventions also often succeed and do a great deal of good.

7

SOCIAL JUSTICE AND THE POOR

75. What is social justice?

Social justice, or distributive justice, is a moral standard by which some people judge political and economic institutions. Advocates of social justice believe the moral justification of our institutions depends on how well these institutions serve the interests of the poor and least advantaged. The basic institutions of society must sufficiently benefit all, including the least advantaged and most vulnerable members of society.

76. Do most libertarians reject social justice?

"Hard libertarians" (see question 5) reject social justice. In their view, justice only requires that people respect one another's rights.

Hard libertarians tend to assume that a commitment to social justice entails a commitment to a welfare state that redistributes wealth. The hard libertarian philosopher Robert Nozick argues that we cannot ask *how* we should distribute wealth unless we have the *right* to distribute it. Suppose you find a lost wallet. Justice requires that you return the wallet to its owner. You shouldn't worry about what's the best way to distribute the money—the money is not yours to distribute.

Nozick says this applies to governments as well. Nozick says that we live in a world with a history. People have prior claims over their wealth. This limits the degree to which anyone—whether a philosopher or a government—can talk about redistributing wealth in order to realize social justice. If people acquire their wealth through force or fraud, they don't have any claim on it. But, he argues, if people acquire their wealth through just means, then no one else has the right to take it from them to give to others. If I rightfully own my property, then the government may not confiscate that property from me, even to help the poor.

The Left often uses the term "distributive justice" as a synonym for "social justice." Nozick says the term "distributive justice" connotes that wealth is like manna fallen from heaven, and that the government's job is to figure out how to distribute the manna. Talk of there being a "distribution of wealth" is misleading: It suggests that *someone* distributed the wealth.

Nozick says that in a free market, there is no more of a distribution of wealth in society than there is a distribution of sexual partners, spouses, or friends. As a matter of fact, some people have more and better friends than others. Some people have more and better sex with more desirable partners than others. We might feel bad for the people who do badly. Still, it makes no sense to talk about fair or unfair distributions of sexual partners, spouses, or friends. No one distributed the partners or friends, so no one distributed them fairly or unfairly. The "distribution" of friends and partners is just whatever pattern happens to result from free people making free choices about whom they will associate with and on what terms.

When people make these choices, some benefit more than others. Some do not benefit at all. But there is no question about redistributing friends, spouses, or sexual partners. No one advocates making supermodels sleep with 40-year-old virgins in order to correct unfair distributions of hot sex. People are entitled to do as they please with their bodies and are entitled to choose whom to associate with, regardless of whether this makes some worse off than others. Even if you think it would be better if everyone had equal access to good sex, you have no right to redistribute sexual access.

Nozick extends this reasoning to questions about the "distribution" of wealth. People are entitled to hold, use, and trade certain kinds of wealth and property. When they make voluntary choices with their wealth, some gain more than others, just like when people make voluntary choices about sex or friendship, some gain more than others.

Nozick argues that justice is not about the *ratio* of wealth. So, for example, suppose in some society, the top 1% have 100 times the income of the bottom 10%. This fact alone tells us *nothing* about whether that society is just or unjust. To know whether the distribution of wealth is just or unjust, we need more information.

What information do we need? Nozick argues that justice is about *how* people acquire their wealth. We need to know how and why people have the income they have. To determine whether the distribution of wealth is just, we need to look at history. If people acquire their wealth in just ways, they are entitled to it. Otherwise, they are not.

When inequality results from free people making free choices over how to use their own property, then the inequality is justified. For example, suppose we each choose to pay Lebron James 25 cents per basketball game to watch him play. Suppose Lebron James thus becomes 100 times richer than the rest of us. Nozick says that there is no injustice here. We were entitled to give our money to James. James was entitled to accept it.

Nozick argues that we should not try to make the distribution of wealth fit some preconceived pattern. Instead, we should ensure that people only acquire wealth through just *procedures*. Nozick calls his theory of distributive justice the *entitlement theory*. It has three main principles:

1. *The principle of justice in acquisition*: Some principle or set of principles that explains how a person may justly

come to own property that was not previously owned. (For example, farming an unowned plot of land may give a person a claim on it.)

2. *The principle of justice in transfer*: Some principle or set of principles that explains how people may come to own property that was previously owned by others. (For example, if I buy your computer, then I justly acquire the computer, and you justly acquire some money.)

3. *The principle of justice in rectification*: Some principle or set of principles that explains what to do when people violate principles 1 and 2. (For example, if I purchase a stolen car, then, even if I didn't know the car was stolen, I should return the car to its rightful owner.)

In summary, the entitlement theory says whatever distribution of wealth arises from a just situation through just steps is itself just.

Critics suspect that the entitlement theory is meant to justify the inequality we see in the real world. Not so. The entitlement theory says that if the history of acquisitions and transfers is just, then the current distribution is just. But, of course, the history of acquisitions and transfers has been highly unjust. Much of the land we own was seized by conquest from people who had themselves seized it through conquest. In our current economy, corporations use government to game the economic system for their own advantage. Big businesses receive bailouts, subsidies, and loans from governments and use the power of eminent domain to seize land and property from the poor to their own benefit. Congresspeople funnel federal money toward their personal projects. And so on.

Thus, Nozick's entitlement theory does *not* justify current inequalities, because current inequalities did not arise through just steps. Nozick even says we may have to redistribute some wealth now in order to rectify past injustices.

Some anti-libertarians say Nozick just assumes people have the right to acquire wealth for themselves no matter what the consequences may be. Contrary to Nozick, they see property rights as sets of conventions. In their view, these conventions can be justified only if everyone subject to them is expected to benefit sufficiently.

77. Do all libertarians reject social justice?

Classical liberals advocated markets in large part to help the poor. Adam Smith said the wealth of nations should be measured not by the size of the king's treasury but by the fullness of the common person's stomach and the opportunities available for his children.

Neoclassical liberals believe just social institutions must tend to benefit all, especially the most vulnerable members of society. Neoclassical liberals believe that liberal market societies are the best means to realize the goals of social justice. Libertarians advocate a high-growth free-market economy—with minimal barriers to entry, few or no immigration and labor restrictions, and little regulation—because they regard this as the way to fight poverty.

Neoclassical liberals agree with hard libertarians that everyone has a right to acquire and use property. However, they add that reasonable people dispute the exact nature and scope of property rights. Property rights are sets of conventions, and there are many different conventions any group of people could live under. (For instance, consider the question of just how long a person can go without using his land before he forfeits his rights to it and it reverts back to being unowned. Or, consider the question of just what an individual needs to do to claim unowned property as his own.) Neoclassical liberals say that it would be unreasonable to demand that everyone accept and abide by these conventions unless they had a sufficient stake in them. Thus, if one set of property rights conventions tended to immiserate the poor or leave innocent people without any wealth or opportunity, that would be reason to reject those property right conventions.

Libertarians add: Even if the point of government is to pro-mote the general welfare, this does not imply we should have a welfare state. A government might try to promote welfare directly, by creating welfare offices, offering subsides, provid-ing basic income, providing tax-subsidized health care, promot-ing or providing employment, and attempting macroeconomic adjustments. Or, a government might try to promote welfare indirectly, by providing a basic institutional framework—such as the rule of law, representative democracy, courts, and a well-functioning property rights regime—within which people will spontaneously act in ways that promote the general welfare.

It's an open empirical question about how much promoting the general welfare depends on direct methods. But there is no question that promoting the welfare depends greatly upon these indirect methods. The average person today is 20 to 30 times richer than the average person 200 years ago. The wealth we now enjoy wasn't just moved around by government trans-fers. It was created by market economies. (The United States today has an economic output greater than the entire world's output in 1950.)

78. What do libertarians think about economic inequality?

Libertarians generally believe that when inequality results from free people making free choices over how to use their own property, then the inequality is justified.

This does not mean that libertarians believe all or even any existing inequalities are therefore just. For instance, Archer Daniels Midland (ADM) lobbies the government for corn sub-sidies. ADM makes money because the government rigs the market in its favor. ADM exploits consumers and taxpayers. Libertarians say that when people acquire wealth through unjust means, they are not entitled to that wealth. However, the problem is not about income or wealth *inequality* per se.

The problem with ADM is not that it has more than others, but that it got its money the wrong way.

Material egalitarianism is the doctrine that everyone ought to possess the same level of income or wealth. Few people really advocate material egalitarianism. If material egalitarianism were true, then it would be better for everyone to be equally poor than for everyone to be rich but unequal. However, it's better for everyone to be rich but unequal than for everyone to be equal and poor. Thus, material egalitarianism is false.

Most reflective people on the left now reject strict material egalitarianism. Nevertheless, they continue to recognize some pull toward material egalitarianism. In particular, they tend to regard material equality as a baseline from which all departures must be justified.

Libertarians of all stripes are unambiguous in rejecting material egalitarianism. On their view, in most situations, material egalitarianism has no moral pull in itself. Imagine two societies, A and B. In both societies, the civil, political, and economic liberties are fully protected, everyone enjoys ample opportunities, everyone has enough, and everyone has high levels of welfare. However, suppose B is more equal than A in its distribution of income or wealth. Most left liberals would favor B over A. Libertarians would be indifferent between them.

Libertarians believe there is no moral remainder to material egalitarianism: It is not (normally) a baseline from which departures must be justified, nor is it morally desirable all things being equal. Libertarians say material egalitarianism misses the point of social justice.

A material egalitarian might say, "Some are rich and some are poor, so we should try to be more equal." In contrast, libertarians say, "The problem isn't that some people have *more*; it's that some people don't have *enough*. The poor of the third world die of starvation and disease, not inequality." Classical and neoclassical liberals are not material egalitarians, but are instead *welfarists*, *sufficientarians*, and/or *prioritarians*.

Welfarism holds that part of what justifies social institutions is that they promote most people's welfare. (Whether a commitment to welfarism in turn suggests a commitment to a welfare state depends in part on what degree a welfare state, as compared to the alternatives, actually succeeds in promoting welfare.) Sufficientarianism holds that all people should have *enough* to lead minimally decent lives. Neoclassical liberals advocate libertarian institutions in part because they believe these institutions will tend to make sure people have enough. Prioritarianism holds that when considering changes to current institutions, all things being equal, we should give more weight to the interests of the worst off members of society.

Classical and neoclassical liberals hold that welfarism, sufficientarianism, and prioritarianism capture all of the moral force of egalitarianism. If welfarist, sufficientarian, and prioritarian goals have been met, from the standpoint of social justice, egalitarianism has no remaining attraction. Neoclassical liberals agree that a fair and just society gives everyone a stake in that society. A just society has institutions that ensure, as much as possible, that everyone has the resources needed to be a free person. Still, they say, the goal of society is to make everyone well off, not to make them equal.

Libertarians want everyone to have an extensive sphere of economic liberty. The Left believes that economic freedom causes income inequality. Libertarians respond in part by saying income equality, in itself, doesn't matter. However, many libertarians also argue that there is no measurable relationship between economic freedom and inequality. For instance, the *Wall Street Journal* and Heritage Foundation annually rank countries by their level of economic freedom. If we graph countries' economic freedom scores against their Gini coefficients (a statistical measure of income inequality), we find no significant relationship between the two. Switzerland, Singapore, Australia, Canada, and New Zealand each have both higher levels of income equality and higher levels of economic freedom than the United States.

79. Why do libertarians oppose welfare states?

The Left tends to think that, without an extensive welfare state, the bottom quartile of people will be left behind. They assume that because libertarians tend to oppose having an extensive welfare state (and many oppose having any welfare programs), libertarians must be callous and indifferent to suffering. They assume libertarians just do not care about the poor. Not so.

Instead, most libertarians dispute that welfare states work as well as the Left believes they do. Or, they claim that there are better alternatives. The Left wants to rescue the poor with welfare programs. Libertarians want to enrich the poor through high-growth economies.

Libertarians believe welfare states often suffer from government failures. (See questions 36 and 37.) They think that welfare states transfer money not to the truly needy and desperate, but instead to strong voting blocs. So, for instance, the elderly are high status in American society. Unwed teenage mothers are low status. The American welfare state does more to help the relatively wealthy elderly than unwed teenage mothers. You might think: This just shows we need to fix the welfare state. Libertarians say, "Good luck with that." Politicians have little incentive to fix this problem.

Libertarians worry that welfare states create perverse incentives and poverty traps. For instance, the field of behavioral economics (the empirical study of economic decision making) shows us that most people underestimate the costs and overestimate the benefits of their bad decisions. It also shows that the poor and uneducated are especially prone to this problem. The economist Bryan Caplan says that if so, when the state offers welfare programs designed to rescue people from their bad choices, it at the same time makes it more likely they will make these bad choices and need to be rescued.

Some libertarians claim welfare states are unfair. Welfare states often transfer money from the conscientious and responsible to the unconscientious and irresponsible. So, for instance, I set aside money for my retirement. I thereby forego current consumption and neglect many of my desires. Many poor retirees who now demand welfare could have done the same but chose not to. They lack means to support themselves because they were irresponsible. They blew their money on new cars, vacations, and other things they did not need. When they retire indigent, they should not demand that *other* working people provide for them. If the ant saves food for winter while the grasshopper plays, when winter comes, the hungry grasshopper has no right to demand the ant feed him.

Note that many libertarians have a nuanced view about irresponsibility. Suppose a 15-year-old girl forgoes (cheap and easily available) birth control, gets pregnant, and cannot support herself or her baby. She may have a stronger than normal claim to be rescued. (Certainly her baby is innocent.) She is not a full adult and not fully responsible. She made poor choices, but unlike retirees who didn't save for retirement, she didn't spend her entire adult life making unconscientious choices.

Most libertarians believe we should be charitable to others. However, our moral duties to provide charity and to rescue others are usually not enforceable. For instance, suppose my parents have money trouble. Even if I should help them, the state may not *force* me to help. Or, suppose my friend needs a ride from the airport. Even if I should help him, the state may not *force* me to help. Some libertarians argue that if the state may not force us to rescue our parents or our friends, then the state certainly may not force us to rescue distant strangers.

80. How can you be a welfarist without advocating a welfare state?

Welfarism is the thesis that part of what justifies social institutions is that they promote most people's welfare. Whether a commitment to welfarism in turn requires a commitment to a welfare state depends on what degree a welfare state, as compared to the alternatives, actually succeeds in promoting welfare.

Being committed to making sure everyone gets enough does not automatically entail a commitment to a strong welfare state. Do we want government to issue legal guarantees that people will achieve a certain level of welfare? Libertarians say this depends on what actually happens when government issues those guarantees and tries to fulfill them. It depends on how competent government is to fulfill those guarantees. It depends on how people react to the guarantees. There is a difference between guaranteeing in the sense of *rendering something inevitable* (as when an economist says that quadrupling the minimum wage would guarantee widespread unemployment) versus guaranteeing as *expressing a firm commitment* to achieve a goal (as when the Bush administration guaranteed no child would be left behind).

Libertarians say that guaranteeing something in the latter sense is no real guarantee. Many things can and do disrupt, corrupt, or pervert legal guarantees. Legal guarantees are good only when they work. If we give government the power to promote some valuable end, there's no guarantee that those in power will exercise it competently, and thus succeed in promoting that end. There's also no guarantee that the people in government will use that power for the intended end, rather than for some private purposes of their own. There is also no guarantee that people will not *take advantage* of the guarantee. For instance, imagine we tried to guarantee everyone $100,000 a year in income. If we did, so many people would leave the workforce that we would not have the tax revenues to pay the guarantee.

Finally, there is no guarantee that such legal guarantees will outperform *other* ways of generating the preferred goal. Libertarians believe many welfare programs work worse than their supporters claim. They believe many welfare programs redistribute wealth toward the well-to-do and well-connected rather than toward the poor.

Libertarians add that regardless of how we evaluate the effectiveness of such programs, welfare programs are not the primary reason the people of the West are as rich as they now are. The West got rich because it had a good mix of stable institutions and relatively high economic freedom. That system unleashed human creativity in ways that made everyone rich. Poor, middle-class, and rich Americans are each much richer than their counterparts 100 or 200 years ago.

Libertarians thus say that in the long term, helping the poor is not about giving them handouts. It is about expanding their available range of opportunities available so that they do not need handouts. In the long term, helping the poor requires serious economic growth.

Sophisticated critics respond that while economic growth is of course the solution to poverty in the long term, in the short term, there is no good alternative to state welfare programs. They say libertarians are right to point out how many of these programs fail or are inefficient. However, they argue, it is better to have these imperfect programs than no programs at all.

81. Are all libertarians opposed to the welfare state?

Hard libertarians (see question 5) tend to believe that the welfare state is illegitimate. In their view, to fund a welfare state requires that the state violate people's property rights in order to provide for others. They say that welfare state forces some people to work for others. Hard libertarians believe we have moral duties to provide aid for the desperately poor, but we may not be *forced* or *coerced* into providing such aid.

Note that libertarians do not necessarily reject all aspects of the welfare state. Robert Nozick, a hard libertarian, says that the current distribution of wealth in any given society arose in unjust ways, in ways that violate libertarian principles. (See question 76.) Rectifying this injustice may require a (temporary) welfare state with some redistribution.

Classical liberals and neoclassical liberals take a softer line. They believe the legitimacy of social institutions depends in part on how well those institutions benefit all, including the most vulnerable members of society. They say that a regime of private property and free markets could not be legitimate if it routinely left large numbers of people desperate and destitute through no fault of their own. Thus, for them, the extent to which a society may have a welfare state depends in significant part on how well markets work and how well the welfare state works.

F. A. Hayek, Milton Friedman, and John Tomasi, among others, each advocate some form of guaranteed income for the desperately poor. However, classical and neoclassical liberals do not envision the state taking control of people's finances, nor do they advocate having a state make sure everyone is "all tucked in" from birth to death. Instead, they believe welfare functions of the state should be minimized.

Classical liberals and neoclassical liberals will sometimes advocate certain welfare state functions, but this does not mean they advocate full-blown "social democracy." They distinguish between a welfare state, which provides social insurance, and an administrative state, which tries to regulate and manage the economy. They believe that while welfare states can be abused and run poorly, administrative states are heavily prone to abuse. (See questions 36, 37, and 74.)

Consider countries such as Denmark or Switzerland, which have effectively separated their welfare state from the administrative state. The *Wall Street Journal* and Heritage Foundation annually rank countries by their level of economic freedom. On nearly every measure associated with the administrative state (such as business freedom, trade freedom, investment freedom, and property rights), Denmark rates as having much higher levels of economic freedom than the United States. Yet Denmark also has a remarkably effective welfare state. Hard libertarians would regard Denmark as unjust because it taxes some to provide for others. Neoclassical and classical liberals in contrast may look favorably upon Denmark or Switzerland.

82. How do libertarians propose to end poverty without an extensive welfare state?

Libertarians believe open and free immigration would help alleviate the world's most severe poverty. (See question 86.) Economists conduct studies to estimate the costs of international barriers on labor mobility (i.e., immigration restrictions). On average, they estimate that eliminating immigration restrictions would *double* world GDP. Poor immigrants would gain the most. Economist Michael Clemens jokes that we have "trillion dollar bills lying on the sidewalk." (If eliminating immigration restrictions really would double world GDP, then these restrictions cost the world $65 trillion.)

The main way libertarians propose to end remaining poverty is to continue doing the thing that has ended poverty in previous eras. As late as 1800 AD, the average person lived on a dollar a day. However, the West grew rich (and, later, much of the rest of the world followed) because it found a good mix of open markets, the rule of law, respect for private property, cultures of tolerance, and other institutions that enabled prosperity to grow. Even today, people around the world (such as in China) lift themselves out of poverty not through redistribution, but because of economic growth.

One way to understand the value of growth is to imagine what would have happened in its absence. Using data from the Bureau of Economic Analysis (BEA), we can estimate that the average growth rate of US real GDP from 1929 through 2004 was about 3.559%. Imagine we had done something to slow this rate of growth by 1 point on average, so that the average growth rate was instead 2.559%. According to the BEA, actual US GDP, in 2000 dollars, was $10,841.9 billion in 2004. The GDP of the United States, with its slower average growth rate of 2.559%, would have been approximately $5,756.4 billion. (At 2% average annual growth, its GDP would be less than $4,000 billion.) If the American economy were less than half its current size, that would hardly help the average poor person, no matter how much redistribution there was.

Redistribution can sometimes help the poor. But redistribution is a short-term solution to poverty at best. Suppose we liquidated all of the wealth (income, stock, land holdings, and all other assets) of the 400 richest people in America. Suppose we then distributed that money equally among the bottom 30% of Americans. We could give each of them a one-time grant of about $15,000. No doubt such a grant would help them in the short run. For some, this would make a huge difference. But that would not be a long-term solution to poverty. The long-term solution is to find a way to grow the economy such that the poorest of the poor are making an extra $15,000 to $30,000 per year on their own.

Anti-libertarians on the left generally agree that growth is essential to ending poverty. However, they argue, as an empirical matter, we will need a welfare state of some sort to ensure that everyone benefits from this growth. (Note that some classical and neoclassical liberals agree.)

83. Why do libertarians claim that governments tend to hurt the poor?

Libertarians believe governments actively harm the poor by

- Imposing licensing schemes and heavy regulations on small businesses, which makes it expensive and close to impossible for the urban poor to open their own businesses
- Providing subsidies and monopoly privileges to the well-connected and rich, thus giving them an even greater advantage on the market against small businesses and the poor

- Creating subsidies in order to help agribusiness, when such subsidies drive up the cost of food and basic goods that the poor consume, goods that eat up a disproportionate share of the poor's income
- Waging the drug war, which is disproportionately fought against poor minorities (though minorities do not use drugs more than whites), and which has had the result of ghettoizing inner cities and creating dysfunctional urban cultures that in turn tend to make the poor more likely to become criminals (see question 50)
- Engaging in "smart growth" urban planning, which tends to drive up the prices of homes, apartments, services, and goods in cities
- Placing heavy restrictions on immigration, thus forcing the world's poorest of the poor to stay put, suffer, and starve, and to be subjected to exploitation and abuse (see question 86)
- Placing price controls, such as minimum wage and rent control laws, which then create shortages of jobs and housing
- Overregulating, when the costs of compliance with regulation fall disproportionately on small businesses, as they must spend much more money per worker to comply with regulations than large corporations do (see question 71)
- Providing the poor with terrible schools, forcing good students to be stuck with terrible teachers and with peers who teach them dysfunctional social norms, caving in to teachers' unions and being unwilling to fire the worst teachers, and being unwilling to provide vouchers for students to attend well-functioning and disciplined private or parochial schools
- Creating welfare programs that create "moral hazard," that is, in which people cannot risk getting a job and supporting themselves for fear of losing their benefits, and so they become dependent on the state

Libertarians say the United States has a large welfare state and spends large sums trying to help the poor. However, they believe the US government acts more like the *enemy* than friend of the poor. The government pays off the poor, but only after it keeps them down.

In response, sophisticated left-liberals, conservatives, socialists, or others might agree that governments often make bad choices that undermine the poor. However, they say, we cannot *blame* poverty on government. Government helps more than it hurts. And, even if it hurts, the solution is to get it to help more, not just to get it to stop hurting.

So, for instance, the progressive Left might agree that inner-city public schools produce poor results. However, they claim there is no better alternative. (See question 90.)

It would take too much space to discuss each of the previous bullet points at length. But here are some examples libertarians might give:

- An African American woman might lift herself out of poverty by offering eyebrow threading or hair weave services. However, she faces zoning restrictions plus rules requiring her to attend expensive (and irrelevant) hairdressing classes and to acquire an expensive (and irrelevant) hairdressing license. And so, the laws prevent her from supporting herself and thus leave her desperate and dependent.
- Another poor inner-city African American might want to provide a service shuttling customers around his part of town, a great opportunity given that the taxis stay away. However, he will not be able to do so without obtaining a taxi license, and taxi licenses are often prohibitively expensive to acquire. The government limits the number of licenses, and in many cities, licenses cost more than $100,000.
- Or, a group of poor Jewish immigrants might band together to create a *tontine*—a communal annuity and

social insurance scheme in which all members pay in and receive death and old-age benefits. However, private insurance companies have, in the past, lobbied the government to outlaw such practices, in order to force the poor to buy private insurance. (The result: The poor often end up stuck with government social insurance.)

- Or, a group of factory workers might band together to hire a doctor to provide health services at a reduced cost to all members. In fact, this was common practice in the past. However, in the past, the American Medical Association faced competition from these "lodge doctors" and then lobbied the government to create a series of regulations that destroyed such practices.

84. Why do libertarians oppose minimum wage laws?

Textbook microeconomics claims that minimum wage laws cause unemployment among the poor and unskilled. If this is correct, then libertarians think that's sufficient reason to reject minimum wage laws.

The market price of a good tends to be equivalent to the marginal value of that good. In a competitive market, when a good is worth $6 to customers, it will tend to sell for $6. This applies to labor, too. Textbook economics says that in a free market, employees tend to be paid their *marginal product*. That is, employees get paid close to what they are worth to employers. If a worker produces $6/hour worth of value for others through her labor, then she will tend to make just under $6/hour.

In general, when a government sets prices *below* the market price, this tends to create a shortage. Customers demand more than suppliers are willing to supply. (For example, when the US government set caps on gasoline prices in the 1970s, this caused a massive shortage.) When government sets prices *above* the market price, this tends to create a glut or surplus. Suppliers offer more than customers are willing to buy.

Wages are just the price of units of labor. If the government makes a law saying that the price of labor must be higher than the market price, this tends to cause a glut or surplus of labor. We call that glut *unemployment.*

Imagine the government passed a law saying that no one could hire a janitor at less than $1 million/year. This law would not turn *any* janitors into millionaires. It would put janitors out of work. It would create a black market in janitorial services. It would induce employers to have secretaries and office assistants do janitorial work on the side.

Suppose a janitor is worth only $5/hour to my company. A competitive free market pressures me to pay the janitor just under $5. Suppose the government requires me to pay the janitor $15/hour. This means every hour I employ the janitor, I lose $10. You can guess how long I'd like to keep him.

The economists William Evan and David Macpherson argue that minimum wage laws hurt poor African Americans more than they hurt poor whites. Consider the least skilled group of workers: 16- to 24-year-olds who lack a high school diploma. Evan and Macpherson argue that increasing the minimum wage by 10% tends to cause about a 2.5% drop in employment for white males in this demographic. However, it tends to cause a 6.5% drop in employment for black males.

Wal-Mart hires many unskilled workers. Unskilled workers are relatively unproductive, and their labor is worth little. Wal-Mart pays them little. Suppose Wal-Mart decided to pay all of its employees at least $20/hour, nationwide. In the short term, that might help the people who currently work at Wal-Mart. But in the long term, this policy is unlikely to make the least skilled workers rich. If Wal-Mart started to pay high wages, Wal-Mart jobs would become attractive to skilled workers. People who currently work as medical assistants or car mechanics would want Wal-Mart jobs. Since they are more productive and have more skills—since their labor is worth more—they will outcompete the kind of people who currently work at Wal-Mart. So, raising wages above market levels is unlikely to help the least skilled workers. Instead, it causes *job gentrification*. (Imagine if Wal-Mart offered to pay its workers $100/hr. Then many of my colleagues would consider becoming Wal-Mart cashiers.)

Some on the left claim that low wages are exploitative. They want to make this exploitation illegal. They say, if minimum wage laws put the least productive workers out of work, so be it. We could just give them welfare checks as compensation.

However, libertarians think this response is far less humane than it looks. Even with welfare benefits, unemployment undercuts people's sense of self-worth. Most people want to feel like productive members of society who pay their own way. Most do not want to feel dependent on society. Joblessness is bad for people's mental health. The unemployed (especially unemployed men) are much more likely to suffer from depression.

Many economists argue that minimum wage laws at least do not cause huge losses in efficiency. For instance, France has high minimum wage laws, while the United States has low minimum wage laws. French worker productivity is still about 85% of American worker productivity. However, this is not surprising. When minimum wage laws are high, this *excludes* the least productive members of society from the market. Minimum wage laws make employers lose money when they hire the least productive workers. Thus, minimum wage laws induce employers to hire high-productivity workers, or to restructure their businesses and use more capital instead of labor.

Many people—even many economists—agree that the minimum wage hurts the poor but advocate the minimum wage anyway. They say such laws express our commitment to the poor. Libertarians find this perverse. They say that if you want to express your commitment to the poor, you don't pass a law that you expect to hurt them. If you do, then you are not actually committed to helping the poor. As the philosopher David Schmidtz says, if your main goal is to show that your heart is in the right place, then your heart is not in the right place.

85. Do libertarians support international aid?

Libertarians respond that this is the wrong question. If we really want to help the rest of the world, we shouldn't open our wallets to provide foreign aid. We should instead open our borders to allow free immigration.

Immigration restrictions prevent labor from moving where it is needed most. They distort the world economy—in fact, immigration restrictions may be the single most inefficient policy governments implement. When economists estimate the welfare losses from immigration restrictions, they tend to conclude that eliminating immigration restrictions would *double* world GDP. The poorest immigrants would benefit the most. The families and friends they leave behind would see large gains. (Immigrant workers remit money back home.)

Even if foreign aid worked, it has no potential to double world GDP. But foreign aid often doesn't work (or at least hasn't worked). (This appears to be the consensus among most economists, not just libertarians.) First world governments send money to third world governments. Third world leaders tend to take the money to support their own and their supporters' interests, rather than their people's interests. When a dictator knows Washington will pay his bills, he can get away with an incompetent or negligent government. He doesn't need his people's support. Foreign aid subsidizes government corruption.

Foreign aid to the third world has no history of success. Since World War II, the first world has given Africa about $1 trillion, and yet incomes in Sub-Saharan Africa are lower today than 40 years ago.

8

CONTEMPORARY PROBLEMS

86. What would libertarians do about illegal immigrants?

Libertarians would grant amnesty to undocumented immigrants. They advocate open borders and free immigration.

Libertarians advocate free immigration in part because immigration restrictions are highly inefficient. When economists try to measure the deadweight loss immigration restrictions cause, they typically estimate that eliminating all immigration restrictions would *double* world GDP. That is, we could add another $65 to 70 trillion to the world economy in a few years if only we liberalized immigration laws.

Libertarians do not just say that free immigration would produce good consequences. They also believe that immigration restrictions are pernicious. Libertarians believe immigration restrictions impose poverty, suffering, pain, and death on some of the most vulnerable people in the world.

Philosopher Michael Huemer explains this with a thought experiment: Imagine starving Marvin heads to the market looking for food. Marvin has little to trade. However, suppose there are people at the market willing to trade food for whatever Marvin has. Imagine that unless someone stops him, Marvin will successfully get to the market, make the trade, and eat. However, now imagine that you forcibly prevent Marvin from getting to the market. You post guards to keep him out. The guards continually capture Marvin and turn him away. Marvin can't barter for food. He starves and dies.

In this situation, Huemer says, you have done something morally comparable to killing Marvin. His blood is on your hands.

In another version of the story, imagine Marvin is not starving, but is instead desperately poor. Imagine that if Marvin makes it to the market, he will make some trades and instantly become *10* times richer. Imagine Marvin will be able to send large amounts of money back to his poor village to feed his entire extended family. However, again, you post guards, who turn Marvin away. In this case, you force Marvin to stay poor. It was not your fault Marvin was poor to begin with, but it is your fault he remains poor.

Huemer admonishes us: In these thought experiments, you do not simply *fail to help* Marvin. That is, you are not doing something equivalent to walking by a beggar without donating your spare change. Instead, you *actively hurt* Marvin by using violence to prevent him from making a trade with a willing partner. It is as if you saw someone else offering a beggar $5 to wash a car window, but you scared the beggar and the driver away with your gun.

Libertarians believe immigration restrictions are morally equivalent to keeping Marvin from the market in these thought experiments. Some people in rich countries want to hire poor foreigners. The foreigners want the jobs. These jobs make the difference between life and death or prosperity and poverty. Immigrants to the United States usually see their income rise by an order of magnitude or more—they go from desperately poor to relatively wealthy almost overnight. But the United States and other countries post armed sentries around their markets. They use violence to stop foreigners from making lifesaving or life-changing trades with willing partners. This is morally equivalent to killing the foreigners or forcing them to stay poor.

Many on the left in American and European politics claim to care about the poor. But their hearts bleed for the American and European lower classes—that is, for people who are wealthy by world standards—not for the world's poorest people. Most people on the progressive left actively try to restrain the world's poorest and most vulnerable people from making lifesaving and life-changing trades with willing employers. They thus condemn the world's poor to death and misery. The progressive Left is delighted with me when I donate money to the poor through OxFam. But the Left forbids me from hiring the poor to mow my lawn, even though that helps them more than an OxFam donation.

From the libertarian point of view, if you do not advocate open immigration, any claim to be concerned about social justice or the well-being of the poor is mere pretense.

Libertarians add: Next time you see a person protesting sweatshops, ask the protestor what she thinks about immigration. She probably opposes allowing poor and unskilled immigrants to travel freely in search of work. But when we have an economic system in which everything—financial instruments, money, factories, services—can move freely across borders, *except poor, unskilled labor,* what happens to the poor people who supply unskilled labor? They will not be able to travel in search of opportunities. They will instead be forced to sit and wait for opportunity to find them. It is thus no surprise that the only opportunities that find them involve low wages and sweaty conditions. In short, our immigration laws make the most vulnerable members of the world sitting ducks for exploitation.

Those who defend immigration restrictions might agree that such restrictions appear evil at first glance. However, they argue, the restrictions can be justified. They argue the following:

1. Free immigration would disrupt and destroy native culture.
2. Free immigration reduces the wages of native-born workers.
3. Free immigration would cause high crime.
4. Immigrants will consume too many welfare services.

Libertarians say that even if the first worry were true, it is not a strong enough concern to justify condemning the world's poor to poverty, suffering, and death. Perhaps there is some value in maintaining a distinctive French culture and identity, but it is not valuable enough to justify forcing millions like Marvin to starve. Moreover, libertarians deny that immigrants destroy culture. Instead, they think immigrants add to culture. As economist Bryan Caplan points out, America's cultural centers (such as New York City and Los Angeles) have high immigration. Its "cultural wastelands" (such as North and South Dakota, Alaska, and Alabama) have low immigration. The economist Tyler Cowen might add: Most "native" cultures are themselves the product of past cultural synthesis. The native cultures we want to preserve arose from past movements of people and their ideas.

Libertarians respond to the second worry by pointing out that it flies against the consensus of professional economists who have studied the issue. Numerous economists have studied the effect immigration has on native wages. The *most pessimistic* of these studies tend to conclude that immigration only has a small (<5%) and short-term negative effect on the wages of low-skilled native workers. These negative effects disappear after a few years. Other native workers' wages *increase*. Immigrants do not usually replace native workers; instead, they bring in new skills and produce new jobs. Thus, even on the most pessimistic accounts, immigration *helps* most natives. It hurts only a small minority of natives, and it only hurts them a small amount for a small time. This is hardly enough to justify condemning the Marvins of the world to poverty, suffering, and death. Again, note that this is what the pessimistic studies say. In general, a majority of economists think that immigration *increases* wages for most people.

Libertarians respond to the third complaint by saying that the facts do not back it up. Sociologist Robert Samson found that first-generation Mexican immigrants are only about half as likely to commit violent crimes as third-generation

Americans (of any nationality). The economists Kristin Butcher and Anne Piehl find that immigrants are incarcerated at only one-fifth the rate of the native born. Given that immigrants tend to be poor, we should expect them to commit more crime, yet they do not. Native-born working-class white people—people who themselves tend to oppose free immigration—are much more likely to commit crimes or go to prison than the immigrants they blame for crime. Libertarians conclude: Immigration does not appear to increase crime. Yet, even if allowing free immigration did increase crime, it would have to increase crime dramatically before that would justify condemning the Marvins of the world to poverty, suffering, and death.

Libertarians have a simple response to the fourth objection: If we can't afford to give immigrants welfare benefits, that doesn't mean we should forbid them from immigrating. Instead, it means we should let them immigrate but deny them welfare benefits. However callous that may sound, it is far less callous than forbidding immigration. Either way (whether we let them immigrate or not), we don't pay welfare benefits. Yet, when we allow them to immigrate, we thereby greatly improve their welfare.

87. What would libertarians do about the War on Terror?

Libertarians claim they could win the War on Terror overnight, and at almost no cost. Libertarians would win the War on Terror the way Switzerland and Sweden have won their wars on terror. Switzerland and Sweden are not targets for terrorism because they do not bully the world. If we want to stop Middle Eastern terrorists from targeting the United States, we should stop messing with the Middle East.

Libertarians say: If you want to know why the Iranian government hates America, read the history of American intervention in the Middle East. Read how the United States propped up repressive dictators. Notice that American military bases surround Iran on all sides. Read newspaper reports about the children the US military murders in the pursuit of "strategic interests." For instance, on the day I wrote this paragraph, NATO forces killed at least eight children in Afghanistan. (What would you do if, in the name of fighting terrorism, Russian bombers killed your kids? Might you at least consider devoting your life to revenge?)

George W. Bush says terrorists hate the United States for its freedom. No doubt Islamic fundamentalists do hate tolerant, liberal societies. But there are more tolerant, more liberal, freer societies than the United States, such as Switzerland. Why isn't it a target?

The CIA itself says Islamic terrorists target the United States because the United States meddles in the Middle East. Terrorism is primarily political, not cultural. The United States *provokes* terrorism.

During the 2012 primary races, a political action committee supporting Ron Paul summarized the libertarian position by running the following advertisement:

> Imagine for a moment that somewhere in the middle of Texas there was a large foreign military base, say Chinese or Russian. Imagine that thousands of armed foreign troops were constantly patrolling American streets in military vehicles. Imagine they were here under the auspices of "keeping us safe" or "promoting democracy" or "protecting their strategic interests."
>
> Imagine that they operated outside of US law, and that the Constitution did not apply to them. Imagine that every now and then they made mistakes or acted on bad information and accidentally killed or terrorized innocent Americans, including women and children, most of the time with little to no repercussions or consequences. Imagine that they set up checkpoints on our soil and routinely searched and ransacked entire neighborhoods of homes. Imagine if Americans were fearful of these

foreign troops, and overwhelmingly thought America would be better off without their presence....

The reality is that our military presence on foreign soil is as offensive to the people that live there as armed Chinese troops would be if they were stationed in Texas. We would not stand for it here, but we have had a globe-straddling empire and a very intrusive foreign policy for decades that incites a lot of hatred and resentment towards us.

Perhaps Bush was right. Perhaps Islamic terrorists hate the United States for its freedom. But they do not fly airplanes into our buildings because of our freedom. They fly airplanes into our buildings because we drop bombs on theirs.

Libertarians recognize this is an unpopular view. It requires us to step up and take responsibility for our actions. It forbids us from accepting the lazy, self-congratulating view that America does no wrong.

That is not to say libertarians favor "isolationism." Libertarians want active involvement with the entire world. However, they want goods and services, not troops, to cross borders. They want a military policy focused on protecting the United States from real and imminent threats, not one that creates threats when it attempts to police the world.

Many libertarians say the War on Terror is an overreaction. In the past 50 years, there have been only about 3,500 deaths from terrorism in the United States. The 9/11 attacks cost $30 billion in cleanup, property damage, and lost income to businesses. We might compare these lost lives and financial losses to the War on Terror itself. So far, fighting the War on Terror has killed over 6,000 American soldiers, over 2,000 American contractors, and over 100,000 (maybe even over 200,000) innocent civilians in Afghanistan, Pakistan, and Iraq. The Watson Institute at Brown University estimates the total real monetary costs of the wars at $3 trillion to $4 trillion. It is thus certainly not clear that the War on Terror helps more than it hurts. Political scientist John Mueller and civil engineer Mark Stewart, in a co-authored article, say that to justify the expense of the Homeland Security Administration, the HSA would need to prevent nearly 1700 major terrorist events per year.

Libertarians add: War is the health of the state. Since 9/11, the United States has become increasingly oppressive toward its own people. Obama asserts that he has the right to assassinate American citizens without due process. The United States has effectively suspended habeas corpus and allows US citizens to be detained indefinitely without a trial, provided they are labeled "enemy combatants." Officers of the Transportation Security Administration routinely touch young children's genitals in the name of fighting terror.

88. What would libertarians do about pollution and the environment?

Libertarians say that if you want to encourage people to conserve a resource, you should give them the resource as *property*. (See also question 65.)

When a resource is held in common, everyone has an incentive to overexploit the resource. The ecologist Garret Hardin calls this problem the "tragedy of the commons." The reason ocean fisheries are dying is that all fishermen have every incentive to catch as many fish as they can before their competitors do.

One way to avoid a tragedy of the commons is to divide resources into private property. In the shepherd example, the pasture is unowned. If a shepherd adds extra sheep, he *internalizes* the reward but *externalizes* the cost. If instead each shepherd owned one-tenth of the pasture, then, when he adds an extra sheep, he would internalize both the rewards and the costs. Each shepherd would have an incentive to use his land sustainably. If a few fail to respond to these incentives and misuse their land, they at least only destroy a small plot, rather than an entire pasture.

Property rights can be a solution to certain kinds of pollution and environmental destruction. Property rights give people long-term stakes in resources. Few people dump oil in their own living rooms and pools, but plenty dump oil in public lakes. Maurice McTigue, a former government minister in New Zealand, says New Zealand used to give short-term licenses to foresters to harvest trees. Foresters tended to clear-cut forests. The government wanted to stop clear-cutting but still wanted to allow profitable lumber production. So, the government experimented with giving the lumber companies a kind of property right. It did not sell the forest to logging companies but gave them long-term rights over a portion of the trees in a given area. The result: Companies stopped clear-cutting forests to make cardboard and started selectively harvesting trees to make furniture.

One libertarian solution to overfishing is to instantiate a "catch share" system. Under a catch share system, the stock of fish is not left in the commons. Instead, each fisherman has a right to catch up to a maximal total percentage of the total stock. For fishermen to increase the size of their catch, they need the total stock to increase. Fishermen lose the incentive to overfish and instead gain an incentive to protect the fishery. States and countries that have tried catch share programs have found that these programs are more effective than other ways of preventing overfishing.

Most libertarians agree that property rights will not solve all problems. We cannot convert everything to property. We might not want to convert everything to property even if we could. Some libertarians believe that remaining environmental problems call for government regulation.

89. What would libertarians do about people who cannot afford health care?

For libertarians, there are short-term solutions and long-term solutions.

The most important long-term solution is to make health care relatively *cheaper*, so people can afford to pay for it more easily. Libertarians propose two ways of achieving this end. First, they advocate high-growth economic policies. They want to replace the low-growth, crony capitalist American economy with a high-growth, free-immigration, free-market economy. If people are richer, they can more easily pay for health care. Second, libertarians want to remove government policies that drive up the cost of health care.

Libertarians believe governments make health care expensive. They believe the FDA has an overly risk-averse approval process. It costs on average $1 billion and takes on average 12 years for a new drug to make it to market. So it's no surprise that drugs tend to be expensive.

Governments actively inhibit competition that would push prices down. For instance, governments make it difficult to open new hospitals. Instead of allowing new hospitals to open (and thus create competition, which would lower prices), governments allow them to open only if they can prove the community needs them. A wide range of high-quality, routine medical services could be provided at low cost by people other than doctors or nurses. However, the American Medical Association (AMA) lobbied the government in the early twentieth century to require a medical license to provide these services. (The AMA's explicit reason for doing so—as revealed by their own professional journals—was to protect themselves from competition and thus to obtain monopoly prices on medical care.) Whenever a government restricts competition, high prices result.

Libertarians believe the government also overregulates private health insurance in ways that make it prohibitively expensive. Different states impose rules that prevent insurance companies from competing with one another and thus keep costs high. Companies are required to offer a range of expensive benefits on demand, even if these benefits are not necessary. Duke University health policy analyst

Christopher Conover said that as of 2004, government regulations increase costs in the health care industry by at least $330 billion.

Current forms of health insurance encourage people to overconsume health care and to pass the costs onto others. People pay health insurance premiums up front. Their employers pay most of their premiums for them. At the point of making medical decisions, they do not see the cost, and they pay only a small fraction of the health care they consume.

Imagine my wife is in a coma. Imagine she has almost no chance of waking. Suppose life support costs $3,000 per day (over $1 million per year). If I am a typical American, I will pay almost none of that cost. If I had to bear some significant portion of that cost, I would weigh the costs and benefits more rationally. I might realize it makes no sense to pay $1 million to keep a person in a vegetative state. However, suppose I do not see the cost. Instead, I push the cost of her care onto everyone else who shares my health insurance provider. In that case, I am much more likely to keep her alive for, say, symbolic reasons. Whenever people can push the cost of health care onto others, they will overconsume health care, and the total costs of health care will go up. This is not a small point. This is the main reason health costs are so high.

Few libertarians claim to have good short-term solutions to our health care mess. In the United States, we do not have a free-market health care system. Instead, we have a badly functioning mix of highly regulated, competition-protected private health care and highly regulated public health care. The libertarian prescription to lowering costs is to make sure that providers face real competition.

Some worry that in a free market, there is no way that people with preexisting conditions can get coverage. Not so. As the economist John Cochrane explains, providers could offer "guaranteed renewable" health insurance. Under a guaranteed renewable contract, once you buy health insurance, you also buy the right to continue purchasing that health insurance for the rest of your life. Just like with currently existing private life insurance, the contract forbids the company from raising rates just because you get sicker. Cochrane has written extensively on various ways that free-market health insurance could solve many of our problems, if only the government would let it.

90. What would libertarians do about failing public schools?

Children in rich school districts do better than children in poor school districts. Rich school districts have fancier facilities and spend more money per pupil. Thus, it is tempting to conclude that spending more money on public schools will produce better performance. Yet almost everyone who studies the relationship between spending and performance concludes that higher spending does not cause better performance. Rich school districts are rich because they have rich homeowners as a tax base. Rich homeowners also tend to be better educated and possess more human capital. Because they are better educated and have more human capital, their children tend to be better educated and possess more human capital, and thus perform better in school. It would be easy to throw more money at schools, but libertarians believe that this easy solution is no real solution.

From the libertarian point of view, the American government is practically at war with the children of poor minorities. First, the government wages the War on Drugs and is "tough on crime." Libertarians believe this ghettoizes inner cities. (See questions 47–50.) Second, federal, state, and municipal governments use regulations and licensing in ways that make it difficult for poor minorities to become self-supporting entrepreneurs and business owners. (See question 83.) As a last straw, governments then make poor children go to the country's worst, most violent public schools.

Libertarians believe solving poor performance in inner-city schools requires a mix of programs. First, the government needs to stop policies that actively hurt the poor and keep them poor. (See question 83.) All things equal, the children of the poor do worse, no matter what school they attend.

Second, libertarians believe the government must encourage school choice. Rather than having the government supply low-quality public education, have it pay for students to attend better private, parochial, or charter schools. If you force children coming from low human capital homes only to study with children from other low human capital homes, and you place their schools in gang- and crime-infested areas, you should expect them to fail.

Charter schools are not a panacea, but they have an advantage over other forms of public schooling. Charter schools need to compete to attract students. If one school does better, it attracts more students. Other schools will try to copy it. For instance, consider the BASIS charter schools in Arizona. BASIS does not have competitive admissions—students win seats by lottery. Yet, thanks to excellent teachers and a rigorous curriculum, BASIS students excel in academics. At elite private schools, gifted students from rich backgrounds might take Advanced Placement calculus exams in their senior year of high school. At BASIS, regular students from poor backgrounds pass these exams in their sophomore years.

Libertarians also tend to believe teachers need more autonomy. Libertarians want individual teachers to be free to design their own curricula. They want teachers to be able to experiment. Good experiments will succeed and be copied. Bad experiments will fail, and teachers will try something else. Libertarians don't want central planners in Washington or in state capitals to decide how everyone will be taught. (Question 73 explains why libertarians believe central planning fails.) Libertarians worry that if students are continually made to take standardized tests, teachers will spend much more time teaching for the test than teaching for real learning.

Some libertarians believe teachers unions (the National Education Association [NEA] and the American Federation of Teachers [AFT]) harm the nation's children. The NEA and AFT are powerful lobbies and voting blocs. No Democrat would dare enrage them. The NEA and AFT do what all unions do— they look out for the interests of the union leadership first and their members second. They do this the way all unions do—by posturing as if they are really looking out for their interests of their stakeholders.

The NEA and AFT routinely block attempts to form schools. For instance, in most American school districts, public school teachers get tenure after two or three years. Tenure means incompetent teachers can't be fired. Michelle Rhee, former chancellor of the District of Columbia's public schools, wanted to eliminate tenure so she could fire the worst teachers. Rhee proposed a deal to the DC unions: You let me fire the worst of you, but I pay the best of you huge bonuses and higher salaries. Union leaders refused to allow their members even to vote on the proposal. (A few years later, a heavily watered-down version of the proposal did pass.) The unions wanted pay to be based on seniority, not performance. Most public school teachers sincerely want to help children and to improve education. Yet, libertarians think, their unions won't let them.

91. What would libertarians do about the rise of the Chinese economy?

The main libertarian reaction to the rise of the Chinese economy is to rejoice. Fifty years ago, Mao Zedong forced 40 million or more Chinese people to starve to death. Almost everyone in China was desperately poor. Later, Deng Xiaoping, the de facto leader of China from the late 1970s until 1990, permitted a range of bottom-up reforms. He let local municipalities decide how to invest, allowed foreign investment and capitalist markets in special economic zones, and significantly reprivatized farming. Agricultural and industrial output quickly increased. Though China did not (and hasn't yet) become rich, it went from famines to food surpluses. From a humanitarian point of view, this is wonderful. We should want everyone everywhere to be rich and happy.

Yet most Americans balk. They see the Chinese economy as a dangerous competitor.

This rests on a mistake. As the Nobel laureate economist Paul Krugman says, competitiveness is a dangerous obsession. Nations are not competing firms. Nations do not compete the way Toyota and Honda compete. "We" are not competing with "them."

Economists repeatedly stress—and everyone repeatedly ignores—that international trade is nothing special. From an economic standpoint, increased American trade with China is not much different from increased Virginian trade with Maryland.

Will China "overtake" the US economy? First, do not be fooled by high growth rates. The US economy has never grown as fast as the Chinese economy is growing now. But the US and Chinese economy are different. China experiences what economists call "catch-up growth." It had a poor, isolated, and dysfunctional economy. Now, it can copy good business practices, institutions, and technological innovations used in other countries. It thus grows very quickly. The United States is at the economic frontier. It cannot enjoy catch-up growth. It has no one to catch up to. For it to grow, it cannot copy others. It has to develop new ideas and technologies.

To understand the difference between cutting-edge and catch-up growth, imagine what would happen to the US economy if Star Trek's Vulcans traded us their warp drives and particle generators for our corn. The American economy would grow much faster than the Vulcan economy. The most economically illiterate Vulcans might then complain that the American economy would overtake the Vulcan economy.

Note that the Chinese economy is, overall, still quite small. (And that is too bad, from a libertarian or humanitarian point of view.) China has the second-highest GDP in the world. In absolute terms, China produces more goods and services than any other country except the United States. But China also has a huge population. When we look at China's GDP per capita (the amount it produces per person), it ranks only around 90th among all countries. Comparing Chinese GDP to, say, the Japanese GDP can thus be misleading. It is somewhat like comparing Mississippi to Fairfax County, Virginia (a rich suburban area near DC). The total income of all Mississippians dwarfs the total income of everyone in Fairfax County. However, Mississippi is poor compared to Fairfax County. The median household income in Fairfax County is three times the median household income in Mississippi.

Some Americans fear that if China becomes richer, it will become a greater military threat. However, as the economist Frédéric Bastiat said, if goods do not cross borders, troops will. China is prosperous because it sells stuff to Americans. Economic interdependency *reduces* the probability two countries will go to war, because it increases the amount they have to lose by fighting. This is one reason libertarians favor international trade.

Finally, many Americans worry about the rise of China because they are suspicious of international trade in general. They mistakenly believe that international trade is bad for economies. The vast majority of economists, regardless of whether they lean left, centrist, or right, disagree. (All libertarians favor free trade, but being pro-trade is not a distinctively libertarian view). In the short run, free trade makes almost everyone wealthier, and in the long run, it makes everyone wealthier. When we buy goods from China, they get dollars in return. Actual US dollars are not worth anything in themselves—they are only valuable because they can be exchanged for American goods and services. Thus, the Chinese will either spend those dollars for American goods and services, or they will exchange the dollars for other foreign currencies (e.g., euros). In that case, someone else (whoever traded euros for the dollars) will buy the American goods and services. As economists say, countries pay for imports with exports. Or, imagine the Chinese decide to sit on the dollars forever, or even burn them. That isn't a problem either. However, that is more or less the same as the Chinese giving us valuable televisions and toys in exchange for ugly pieces of paper with pictures of dead presidents.

In early 2012, a Chinese automobile company opened an assembly plant inside Bulgaria, the poorest country in the European Union. China doesn't just "steal jobs" from the first world. It also creates jobs in other countries.

92. Did an unregulated free market cause the recent financial crisis?

Long before others believed in the bubble, libertarians claimed US housing and monetary policies were creating an impending disaster. They were ignored. Then, when the predicted bubble burst, everyone blamed the bubble on an unregulated free market in housing and finance.

The United States has a mixed economy, not a free-market economy. It does not have the freest economy in the world. In fact, many countries that progressives label "social democracies" have freer economies than the United States. (See question 98.) Yet whenever something bad happens in the economy, many people have a knee-jerk reaction: "This proves free-market capitalism fails!"

Almost everyone interprets the 2008 US financial crisis through an ideological lens. People who hate markets look and see what they expect to see: massive market failure caused by stupid and corrupt financiers. People who distrust government look and see what they expect to see: massive government failure caused by stupid and corrupt government regulators.

Libertarians say that whatever stance one takes, one must acknowledge that US financial markets are and were very heavily regulated. (That is compatible with holding that they were regulated badly or not regulated enough.) One has to acknowledge that government deserves at least much of the blame, because it created bad incentives that helped to create the crisis. Perhaps, in the final analysis, the market will bear the most blame. However, if a person complains that an unregulated free market in finance caused the problem, that person isn't making a serious objection.

Under a free-market system, if a bank makes a bad loan, it suffers a financial loss. Banks have an incentive to assess risk properly. That incentive does not guarantee that banks won't make systematic errors. However, libertarians add, the government actively encouraged bankers to underestimate risk and make mistakes.

The economist Russ Roberts says that the government encouraged banks to "gamble with other people's money." He asks us to imagine that you have a business that lends money to smart gamblers. At first, you and the other lenders make lots of money. Yet, imagine the gamblers become reckless and start taking bigger risks. You and the other lenders worry you won't recover your principal. You'd probably stop lending money to the gamblers. You would try to stop the gamblers' risky behavior.

However, suppose your wealthy Uncle Sam is sitting on the sideline, watching the games. Suppose he likes the gambling and encourages it. Suppose—based on his past behavior—you have every reason to think that if the big gamblers go broke, he'll cover their debts. In that case, Roberts says, you and the other lenders would tend to ignore the gamblers' reckless behavior. You would not try to stop them from making risky bets. You would keep lending money even as the bets get riskier and the debts pile up. You might not even bother to increase the interest rate on your loans.

Roberts claims this thought experiment parallels what happened in the financial crisis. The US government credibly committed itself to bailing out big banks that made bad decisions. After all, as former FDIC chairperson Irvine Sprague says, by 1986, in 46 of the 50 largest bank failures in US history, the US government bailed out the banks. No depositor or creditor lost any money in any of these 46 cases. The US government has also repeatedly bailed out large corporations. It has even bailed out other countries.

Financiers thus believed that if they made risky decisions, they could socialize the risk but privatize the benefits. Financiers believed if their risky decisions led to disaster, the US government would bail them out. They were right. In the recent crisis, the government did in fact bail out most of the banks that made stupid decisions.

Parents of irresponsible adult children understand the idea of tough love. For instance, suppose you have a prodigal adult son. He never saves money and always overspends. Suppose if you do not bail him out right now, he will lose his car and apartment. Failing to bail him out allows a disaster in the short term. Still, he will then be forced to stand on his own two feet. He will realize he can't assume you will rescue him. He is less likely to blow all his money again. On other hand, if you bail him out, he has every reason to remain irresponsible. You make it *more likely* he will need another rescue.

When we insulate people from the bad effects of their bad choices, we get more bad choices. When you subsidize something, you get more of it. Libertarians say: So it goes with bad bank decisions. When governments bail out banks, this might help alleviate disasters in the short term. Yet at the same time, this invites more and more disasters to occur in the long term. It makes it more likely the government will have to bail out banks again and again and again.

Libertarians argue that government-sponsored enterprises (GSEs) Fannie Mae and Freddie Mac helped to cause the crisis. Fannie Mae and Freddie Mac buy a large number of risky mortgages from private banks. Private banks write mortgages to low-income and high-risk customers knowing they can then sell the mortgages to the GSEs. The Clinton administration wanted to increase home ownership in the United States. The government instructed Fannie Mae and Freddie Mac to buy ever more risky mortgages from banks. To comply with the Community Reinvestment Act, the GSEs and banks had to provide loans with lower down payments to lower-income borrowers. Banks had incentives to write loans to risky clients, since they could then sell these loans to the GSEs.

Many libertarians warned early on that there was a housing bubble that would lead to a housing crisis. They were ridiculed or ignored. On YouTube, you can watch Ron Paul arguing back in 2003 in Congress that the government was feeding a housing bubble. Throughout his time in office, Paul has asked Fed governors whether government-sponsored credit inflation would induce bad investments and future crises. Each time, the governors would respond that they were competent to manage the economy. The libertarian-leaning Peter Schiff (who heads Euro Pacific Capital) began warning of a bubble in 2002. You can watch him on YouTube appearing on news shows to warn about the bubble, only to be laughed at by interventionist economists and news commentators.

Of course, the cause of the financial crisis is one of the most hotly debated issues in past years. Many intellectually honest economists dispute the libertarian perspective presented here. Some libertarian-leaning thinkers, such as legal theorist Richard Posner, have moved farther away from libertarianism as a result of the crisis.

93. How would libertarians fix the economy?

The US economy has been sluggish for the past 10 years. Yet not every country had bad economic performance over the past decade. The first world countries—such as Australia—that had a good decade kept their economies liberal and free. The first world countries that had a bad decade—such as the United States—reduced economic freedom.

Libertarians think that the United States made bad policy choices that inhibited growth. The way to fix the economy is to stop making these mistakes.

The United States destroys wealth through war. Brown University's Watson Institute for International Affairs estimates that the Afghanistan and Iraq wars will cost the United States nearly $4 trillion. So, this means that through deficit financing and taxation, the US government funnels money from the *productive* parts of the US economy to the *wasteful* and *destructive parts*.

War is not the half of it. Libertarians believe the United States has continued to become a *rent-seeking*, corporatist society. That is, increasingly in the United States, economic success is less about winning customers in a free market and more about winning the favor of Washington. Washington chooses policies that benefit large, well-connected corporations over small but more productive businesses. (See question 71.) The US government takes money from productive enterprises to bail out wealth-destroying but well-connected enterprises, such as General Motors.

Libertarians say that if we want to jumpstart the US economy, we need to make the United States a more attractive place to do business. This means:

- Reduce the red tape, licensing rules, and regulations associated with doing business. It's ECON 101: If you drive up the costs of producing new businesses and new laws, you get lower supply. Right now, according to the US government itself, it costs firms on average almost $11,000 per employee to comply with regulations.
- Reduce the regulations that make it costly to hire new employees. When employers are forced to pay ever more

expensive benefits, unemployment insurance, workers' compensation insurance, and so on, existing employers hire less. Entrepreneurs choose to not start businesses.

- Reduce corporate income taxes. Corporations in the United States have to pay both state and federal income taxes. The combined tax rate—about 40%—is higher than what corporations face in all but two or three other countries in the Organisation for Economic and Co-operative Development (OECD). All things equal, it is more attractive to start businesses elsewhere than here. (Note, however, that US corporate tax rules allow many deductions and loopholes. Big corporations that can afford fancy accountants can save money by doing business in the United States, but only if they devote massive resources into gaming the tax system. That is still wasteful and unproductive.)

- The economist Alex Tabarrok claims that the US patent system inhibits innovation. Companies now spend less time trying to win customers through new innovations and spend more time trying to make competitors lose customers by using frivolous patents against them.

- We need to make it easier for both high- and low-skilled immigrants to join the American economy.

- We need to reform education, so that more students are drawn into science, engineering, and technology, rather than consulting, finance, and law. We also need to reform our political system so that it does not make consulting, finance, and law the quickest way to make a buck.

Many on the left agree with many of these claims—they are not distinctively libertarian. However, they argue, this is not enough. Many left-leaning economists think the government should use "fiscal policy"—that is, increased spending—to jumpstart the sluggish economy.

9

POLITICS: YESTERDAY, TODAY, AND TOMORROW

94. How popular is libertarianism in the United States?

Somewhere between one-tenth and one-third of Americans are libertarians.

Many libertarians do not self-identify as libertarian. They call themselves liberals, moderates, or conservatives. Many of them vote Democrat or Republican.

Thus, to know what percentage of Americans are libertarian, we can't just ask people if they are libertarians.

When researchers want to know how to label a person's political views, they do not ask how that person labels herself. Instead, they ask her a battery of substantive ideological questions. They assign her the label that best fits her substantive political beliefs.

Researchers at the University of Michigan, Stanford University, and elsewhere conduct the American National Election Studies, a study of voter opinion. The surveys ask voters to answer various ideological questions, such as whether we should have more or less government control of the economy or whether we should be more or less tolerant of others with different lifestyles and moral beliefs. Using this data, analysts at the CATO Institute (a libertarian think-tank in Washington, DC) claim that approximately 15% of voters qualify as libertarian.

However, other polls and surveys find a larger percentage of voters who are libertarian or libertarian leaning. Gallup polls generally identify that 20% to 23% of voters are libertarian. A 2007 *Washington Post*-ABC News Poll found that roughly 26% of Americans are libertarian. Libertarians are sometimes described as economic conservatives and social liberals. The CATO Institute recently commissioned Zogby International to survey over 1,000 voters from the 2006 midterm election. The survey asked, among other questions, whether voters regarded themselves as socially liberal and fiscally/economically conservative. Almost 59% of voters labeled themselves as such.

Many libertarian positions are on the rise. In 1988, only about 10% of Americans supported same-sex marriage; now about half do. In 1970, only about 12% of Americans favored legalizing marijuana; now about half do.

Thus, about one-tenth to one-third of American voters are libertarian and libertarian leaning. If these voters were organized around their common beliefs, they could form a powerful voting bloc. However, given the mechanics of the American electoral system, these voters tend to vote, with unease, for anti-libertarian Republicans and Democrats.

95. Is the Tea Party libertarian?

Overall, the Tea Party movement is not libertarian, though it has many libertarian elements, and many libertarians are Tea Partiers.

The Tea Partiers are united by their distrust of Washington politics. They share the libertarian view that DC tends to be corrupt, and that Washington often promotes special interests at the expense of the common good.

However, Tea Party members are predominantly populist, nationalist, social conservatives rather than libertarians. Polls indicate that most Tea Partiers believe government should have an active role in promoting traditional "family values" or conservative Judeo-Christian values. Many of them oppose free trade and open immigration. They tend to favor less government intervention in the domestic economy but more government intervention in international trade. Many Tea Party supporters favor interventionist foreign policy.

Based on survey data, the libertarian magazine *Reason* judges that at most 40% of self-identified Tea Partiers are broadly libertarian. The majority of Tea Partiers are traditional social and economic conservatives.

In an article in *Discover* magazine, Chris Mooney points out that many surveys indicate that Tea Partiers desire to see religion play a strong role in politics. Tea Partiers tend to oppose feminism, abortion rights, immigrant rights, and other libertarian issues in civil liberties. They tend to support stiffer penalties for crime, rather than wanting criminal punishment reform, as libertarians do.

The Tea Party is not a homogenous group. It claims to advocate small government. However, overall, the Tea Party is best seen as a conservative movement. A significant percentage of Tea Partiers may be libertarian leaning, though only a small percentage of libertarians have any affiliation with the Tea Party.

96. Is Occupy Wall Street libertarian?

The Occupy Wall Street movement is not libertarian overall, though libertarians and occupiers do share some common grounds.

Occupiers, like libertarians, oppose the government–big business alliance. However, most occupiers want to reduce corporatism and crony capitalism by increasing government power over the economy. Libertarians believe that increasing government power over the economy will increase corporatism and crony capitalism. (See question 71.)

Occupiers generally are radical participatory democrats who oppose market economies, private property, and free trade. In these respects, occupiers are anti-libertarian.

However, occupiers tend to oppose the Patriot Act, the Bush–Obama wars, militarism, the War on Drugs, and government curtailment of civil liberties. In these respects, libertarians and occupiers overlap.

97. Are most libertarians members of the Libertarian Party?

No. Many libertarians are apolitical. They do not vote or join political causes. Most politically active libertarians vote either for Republicans or Democrats rather than for third parties. The CATO Institute claims, using polling data from Zogby International, that less than 20% of libertarians voted for a third party in either the 2004 or 2006 elections. Libertarians are more likely to vote Republican than Democrat, though in recent years, this trend has been reversing. (In particular, many libertarians voted for Obama in 2008. They hoped a Democrat would be less militaristic and more respectful of civil liberties than a Republican.)

98. Is the United States the most libertarian country?

No. Even though the United States has the highest number (in both absolute and percentage terms) of self-identified libertarians, and even though libertarian ideas get more play in mainstream US politics, the United States is not the most libertarian country overall. It does not have the strongest commitment to economic or to civil liberties. Many of the countries that Americans and others are inclined to describe as "social democracies" or "socialist" actually are more libertarian than the United States.

Libertarian *rhetoric* is more prevalent in the United States than elsewhere. Americans talk about liberty more than others do. Americans often claim that liberty, not equality, community, or social justice, is America's foundational value.

None of this shows that the United States is the most libertarian country. Talking the libertarian talk is not walking the libertarian walk. We need to see which countries have the most libertarian policies. We need to see how well countries protect economic and civil liberties.

The *Wall Street Journal* and Heritage Foundation produce an annual Index of Economic Freedom. They rate countries for their respect for property rights, freedom from corruption, business freedom, labor freedom, monetary freedom, trade freedom, investment freedom, financial freedom, fiscal freedom, and government spending. Hong Kong, Singapore, Australia, New Zealand, Switzerland, Canada, Chile, Mauritius, and Ireland have higher scores than the United States. The United States ranks only 10th overall.

Note that this index may *understate* how anti-libertarian the United States is. After all, the index tends to rank countries lower if governments spend large amounts on social insurance. Yet many classical liberals and neoclassical liberals are not in principle opposed to government social insurance. (See question 5.) Thus, suppose we separate the idea of the *administrative* state, which tries to control, regulate, manipulate, and manage the economy, from the *social insurance* state, which provides tax-financed education, health care, or unemployment insurance. On the Index of Economic Freedom, many countries that rank lower than the United States have far less extensive administrative states than the United States. For instance, Denmark ranks much higher than the United States on property rights, freedom from corruption, business freedom, monetary freedom, trade freedom, investment freedom, and financial freedom. Luxembourg, the Netherlands, the United Kingdom, and many other countries beat the United States on these measures as well. Thus, many other European countries might reasonably be considered more economically libertarian than the United States.

The Fraser Institute publishes an annual Economic Freedom of the World Report, which also ranks countries by their commitment to economic freedom. Their results are similar to the *Wall Street Journal* results. The United States ranks 10th overall. Australia, New Zealand, the United Kingdom, Canada, and Switzerland have higher levels of economic freedom. Many of the Scandinavian countries—which Americans often call "socialist"—beat the United States on many central aspects of economic freedom.

Thus, the United States is not the most economically libertarian country.

It is most likely not the most civil libertarian country either. In this case, there are no comparably detailed rankings. For instance, Freedom House ranks countries by their commitment to political and civil liberties, but its rankings are too coarse to differentiate among the Western countries.

However, we can look at a list of issues to make an overall judgment. Australia, Switzerland, Canada, and the United Kingdom probably are more economically libertarian overall than the United States. How do these five countries compare on civil liberties?

Same-sex marriage is legal throughout all of Canada. Same-sex civil unions are legal throughout all of the United Kingdom and Switzerland. In the United States, some states allow same-sex marriage, others allow same-sex civil unions, and others forbid either. The United States has more restrictive drug laws and more militaristic and violent enforcement of these laws than Canada and most European countries.

Two major trends undermine the United States' commitment to civil liberties. First, the United States jails more people than any other country in the world. About 1 out of 100 American adults is behind bars right now. The United States has more prisoners than China, even though China is a communist regime with four times the American population. Second, since 9/11, the United States has become increasingly oppressive toward its own people. Obama asserts that he has the right to assassinate American citizens without due process. The United States has effectively suspended habeas corpus and allows US citizens to be detained indefinitely without a trial, provided they are labeled "enemy combatants."

Worse, the United States routinely harms innocent civilians in other countries. To fight the War on Drugs, it induces South American governments to dump herbicide on peasants' farmland. The United States routinely bullies countries around the world to advance its perceived national interests. So far, the War on Terror has killed over 100,000 (maybe even over 200,000) innocent civilians in Afghanistan, Pakistan, and Iraq.

Thus, overall, New Zealand, Australia, Switzerland, and Canada are more libertarian than the United States. Hong Kong, Denmark, the United Kingdom, and a few other European countries are arguably more libertarian as well.

99. Which states are the most and least libertarian?

The Mercatus Center, a policy institute at George Mason University, publishes a biennial report called "Freedom in the 50 States: An Index of Personal and Economic Freedom." A state gets a low ranking by having paternalistic policies, interfering with citizens' civic and personal liberties, imposing heavy regulations or licensing requirements, and making it difficult to do business.

According to this report, New Hampshire, South Dakota, and Indiana are the freest, most libertarian states. New York, New Jersey, and California are the least free, most authoritarian, least libertarian states. New Hampshire ranks first overall, first in economic freedom, and 11th in personal freedom. New York is 50th overall, 50th in economic freedom, and 48th in personal freedom. Oregon, Vermont, and Nevada have the highest ratings for personal freedom. Maryland, Illinois, and New York have the lowest ratings for personal freedom.

Of course, these rankings need to be taken with a grain of salt. Most people would probably feel freer living in a bohemian neighborhood in Brooklyn than in a small town in Mississippi.

Some critics of libertarianism note that many of the *least* libertarian states, by Mercatus's rankings, are also some of the richest. The Mercatus Institute may hold that economic and personal freedom lead to prosperity, but relatively unfree New York, California, and New Jersey are among the richest US states.

100. Was the United States ever a libertarian country?

Many American revolutionary leaders were classical liberals. However, the United States was never a libertarian country.

Until 1865, slavery was legal in the United States. (In contrast, England abolished slavery in 1833.) Jim Crow laws required discrimination until the late 1960s.

Women had second-class legal status for most of American history. They were denied control of their reproductive rights—and even denied the right to refuse sex from their husbands—for much of US history. Obscenity laws were often used to limit their access to birth control. For instance, the Comstock Law of 1873 criminalized sending "lewd" materials through the mail. The US government wanted to prevent women from mailing contraceptive devices or information about contraception. (However, the law was only weakly enforced. In fact, the contraceptive industry flourished during this time.)

The US government regulated the economy less in the past than it does now. However, the United States has always had a system of tariffs and subsidies. It has always intervened to sponsor well-connected corporations. This was one source of conflict between the North and South. (Abraham Lincoln, for one, hated free trade. He imposed high tariffs right after taking office.) The industrialist North imposed tariffs. This forced the cash-poor South to buy expensive domestic goods rather than cheaper goods from England.

101. Is the United States becoming more or less libertarian?

Women, Jews, African Americans, and most minorities experience more freedom in the United States now than in the past.

Forty-five years ago, blacks were second-class citizens almost everywhere; 160 years ago, they were property.

Women now have access to birth control. They no longer lose the right to say "no" to sex just by saying "I do" to marriage. When women get married, their legal rights are no longer subsumed under their husband's rights. They can keep their children after divorce.

Americans are more tolerant now than in the past. Most Americans find it easier now than ever before to lead lives they regard as their own.

With all that in mind, libertarians worry about recent trends. The United States seems less committed to economic freedom now than in past years. For the past decade, the United States' scores on the Heritage Foundation/*Wall Street Journal* Index of Economic Freedom and on the Frazer Institute's Economic Freedom of the World Report have dropped. The economy is becoming ever more regulated. Business owners face more red tape each year. In 2011, the federal government added over 100,000 pages of new laws and regulations.

Libertarians believe the United States is becoming more and more of a crony capitalist economy. Businesses often make profits not by offering better products than their competitors, but by pressuring governments to intervene on their behalf. Well-connected businesses use subsidies, tariffs, or predatory regulations to push competitors out of the market. The productive and innovative—those who make wealth—are taxed or regulated out of business in order to support those who do not make wealth.

The War on Terror has increased government disregard and abuse of citizens' civil liberties. We now have warrantless surveillance, Guantanamo Bay, and a president who asserts the right to assassinate American citizens. Despite his promises to the contrary, Obama expanded rather than retracted executive power.

However, from a libertarian view, there are some positive trends. More states are decriminalizing marijuana. More states have legalized gay marriage or civil unions than have in the recent past.

102. What could a libertarian president actually do?

Imagine a libertarian were elected president. What would he or she be able to do? This depends on whether the president has congressional support.

If the libertarian president also had a libertarian Congress, she could quickly turn the United States into a libertarian country. Libertarians do not agree on everything. (See question 5.) However, there is more agreement among self-identified libertarians than among committed Democrats or Republicans.

Imagine instead that a libertarian was elected president, but imagine that Congress remained controlled by the Democratic Party. In this case, the libertarian could do much less. A libertarian president could and probably would stop all American wars and foreign intervention almost immediately. He could shut down American military bases oversees and bring troops home. He could end the War on Terror by withdrawing all troops from the Middle East, withdrawing military and financial support of Israel, and apologizing for past US abuses and atrocities.

Congress has delegated much of its rule-making power to federal agencies. These agencies report to the president. The president could issue executive orders to these agencies and demand that they change their policies in a more libertarian direction. He could order the DEA to stop fighting the War on Drugs. (Even if a libertarian president could not just end the drug war, at the very least, he could offer a rubber stamp pardon for anyone convicted of drug offenses or for any other victimless crimes.) He could order the FDA to lessen drug regulations. The president could direct federal agencies to allow in more immigrants with fewer restrictions. However, it is possible that many of the career bureaucrats in these agencies would just ignore the orders. So, it is unclear how much a libertarian president could do.

The president might be able to cut spending by vetoing Congress's proposed budgets. The president could probably reduce the growth of government power by vetoing interventionist or pork barrel legislation. Of course, Congress could override the president's veto. However, Congress can override a veto only with a two-thirds supermajority. They would find it easier to compromise with a libertarian president than to override his veto.

103. Might the United States become libertarian soon?

Overall, libertarians constitute between one-tenth and one-third of American voters. (See question 94.) Most voters flock to the Democratic or Republican parties. If they formed a united coalition, they could exert much more control. Still, unless the median American voter becomes libertarian, the United States is unlikely to become a libertarian country. In recent years, overall, US economic and social policies have been moving away from rather than toward libertarianism. (See question 101.)

However, in many respects, the American public speaks with an increasingly libertarian voice. In recent Gallup polls, a record 82% of Americans believe the country is badly governed. Sixty-nine percent say they have little or no confidence in Congress. Half of Americans view the government as an immediate threat to citizens' rights and freedoms. Even with soaring gas prices and the recent financial crisis, Americans view the gas, banking, and real estate industries more positively than they view their own government.

Recent Gallup polls find that Americans believe the federal government wastes half of every dollar spent. However, this is probably uninformed opinion. Most Americans do not know how the government spends its money. For instance, the typical American thinks that 8% of the federal budget goes to foreign aid, but the real number is about 1%. Thus, Americans might believe the money is wasted only because they do not know how it is spent.

Explicit support for libertarian ideas is on the rise. In a recent CNN poll, a record high of 63% of Americans agreed that the government is doing too much and that more issues should be left to individuals and businesses. Fifty percent said that government should not try to promote traditional values. American citizens increasingly seem to favor less extensive government regulation of the economy and of social issues.

104. What influence does libertarianism have outside the United States?

Many democracies have libertarian or liberal parties, though these parties are often small. There are also free-market or libertarian think tanks and policy institutes throughout the globe, such as the Institute of Economic Affairs and the Adam Smith Institute in the United Kingdom; the Fraser Institute in Canada; the Copenhagen Institute in Denmark; Avenir Suisse, Liberales Institut, and the Institut Constant de Rebecque in Switzerland; Bruno Leoni Institute in Italy; Eudoxa and Timbro in Sweden; the Association for Liberal Thinking in Turkey; the Center for Free Enterprise in South Korea; Libertad y Desarrollo in Chile; Instituto Liberdade in Brazil; and the European Independent Institute in the Netherlands.

Many prominent twentieth-century and contemporary libertarian academics, scholars, and writers come from outside the United States. Novelist Ayn Rand and legal theorists Eugene Volokh and Ilya Somin come from the former USSR. Many free-market-orientated economists were inspired by Austrians, such as Ludwig von Mises or F. A. Hayek. Jagdish Bagwhati and Deepak Lal are from India.

As discussed in question 98, many countries have more libertarian policies, if not more libertarian rhetoric, than the United States. One way to measure the influence of libertarian ideas is simply to measure the extent to which countries tend toward libertarian outcomes.

105. Is the world becoming more or less libertarian?

Overall, the world is moving toward libertarianism, though it is unlikely any country will actually end up being fully libertarian. In general, across the world, economic barriers are coming down. Tolerance for diversity is increasing. Traditionally unfree countries are becoming freer and freer. Even nominally communist countries, such as China, are liberalizing their economies and allowing greater personal liberty. Compare the situation now to 1960. In 1960, more people lived in totalitarian communist regimes or oppressive dictatorships than in liberal democracies.

That said, there are some negative trends. The NGO Freedom House publishes an annual report rating countries by their commitment to political and civil liberties. In their most recent report, they describe 87 countries as free, 60 as partly free, and 48 as not free. In their rankings, things have been getting worse rather than better over the past five years.

As I write, we are in the midst of the "Arab Spring." Protestors have pushed rules out of power in Egypt, Yemen, Libya, and Tunisia. Throughout the Middle East, citizens protest and demand reform. The Arab Spring might result in greater freedom. It might instead lead to greater sectarian violence and civil war. It might lead to oppressive, theocratic democracies. It might just replace the old dictators with new ones. Revolutions usually end badly rather than well. We cannot predict the results.

GLOSSARY

absolute right A right that cannot be overridden or outweighed by other concerns.

anarchism The belief that all governments are inherently unjust, and/or that it is feasible and desirable to live without a government.

authority The power to create new moral obligations in others. A government has authority over others when those others have a moral obligation to obey its commands.

big government A derogatory term for an interventionist government; a government that attempts to manage and control many aspects of people's lives.

capitalism A form of economic organization in which the means of production are privately owned.

civil liberties/rights The right to free speech, right of free assembly, right of association, freedom of conscience, right of bodily integrity and freedom from abuse and assault, freedom of lifestyle choice, right to protest, right to exit (i.e., the right to leave a country and to renounce citizenship), freedom of sexual choice, and right of substantial due process in criminal procedures.

classical liberalism An early, less stringent form of libertarianism that developed in the seventeenth century.

conservative A person who favors having government reinforce traditional modes of life.

corporatism A system in which large corporations have too much control or power over government.

crony capitalism A system in which success on the market depends on seeking and receiving government favors, privileges, subsidies, and tax breaks; a system in which businesses collude with government.

democracy A political system in which all citizens equally share fundamental political power.

economic liberty/rights Rights to own personal private property, to own private property in the means of production, to start and run businesses, to make financial decisions for oneself, and to make trades on one's own terms with willing partners.

egalitarianism The view that all people should have approximately the same income or wealth.

externality A cost or benefit a person imposes on an innocent bystander.

"formal liberty" A derogatory term, used to describe negative liberties that are protected by law, but which may be of little value to the poor.

free market A system in which people are free to make any voluntary trades they wish with willing partners.

GDP Gross domestic product, one formal measurement of a region or country's economic output.

government A subset of a society that claims to (1) have a rightful monopoly on the use of violence, (2) have the right to issue orders and commands to people who live and work within a geographic area, and (3) have the right to use violence and threats of violence to coerce people into complying with these orders and commands.

government failure Occurs when governments produce inefficient or bad outcomes.

hard libertarianism A form of libertarianism that developed in the twentieth century. Hard libertarians believe rights are nearly absolute. They reject social justice and any form of the welfare state.

left-liberal In political philosophy, someone who favors extensive civil rights but not extensive economic liberty; someone who favors social democracy and government intervention into the economy.

legal moralism The view that government should enforce all moral requirements. Legal moralists believe that if something is morally wrong, the law should prohibit it.

legitimacy A government has legitimacy just in case it is permissible for it to create and enforce rules and laws.

liberal In political philosophy, any person who believes liberty is a fundamental value. In American political discourse, a person who advocates left-wing political beliefs.

libertarianism A political philosophy (or set of related political philosophies) that views every person as having an extensive range of civil and economic rights. Libertarians believe people should be permitted to do almost anything they like, provided they do not violate others' equal rights.

liberty Generally, a condition in which a person has control or power over herself. See *negative liberty* and *positive liberty*.

market failure Occurs when markets produce inefficient outcomes.

market society Any economic system organized around free markets and extensive economic rights.

Marxism Any political philosophy derived from or associated with the socialist philosopher Karl Marx. Marxists advocate socialism and believe market societies are repugnant.

material egalitarianism The doctrine that, as a matter of justice, everyone ought to have the same wealth or income.

negative liberty The absence of interference, obstacles, or impediments.

negative right A person has a negative right to X when other people have an enforceable moral obligation not to interfere with that person as she engages in X.

negative-sum game A game in which everyone can or does lose; an interaction in which everyone is made worse off.

neoclassical liberalism A recently developed form of libertarianism that affirms ideals of social justice; sometimes called bleeding heart libertarianism or Arizona School liberalism.

political liberties/rights Rights that give people a share of government power, such as the right to vote, run for office, and hold office if elected.

positive liberty The power or capacity to achieve one's goals.

positive right A person has a positive right to X when others have an enforceable moral obligation to provide her with X.

positive-sum game A game in which everyone can or does win; an interaction in which everyone is made better off.

prima facie right A right that can be overridden or outweighed by other moral concerns.

prioritarianism The view that in justifying social institutions, we must give extra weight to the interests of the worst off and most vulnerable members of society.

property right A right over an external object, which may include the right to exclude others from using it; the right to use it oneself; the right to modify, sell, give away, or destroy the object; and the right to make money by using the object.

psychologism egoism A theory that holds that all voluntary human action is motivated solely by self-interest; a theory that holds that people are never altruistic.

public choice economics A branch of economics that uses economic analysis to explain political behavior; developed the concept of government failure.

rent seeking Occurs when a firm (or union, special interest group, etc.) tries to get a special privilege or benefit from government that benefits the firm but which harms almost everyone else and society as a whole on net.

sufficientarianism The view that for social institutions to be legitimate, they must tend to ensure people have enough to lead decent lives.

social justice To advocate social justice is to believe that for social institutions to be legitimate, they must benefit all members of society, including the worst off. Egalitarianism, welfarism, prioritarianism, and sufficientarianism are some different conceptions of social justice.

socialism An economic system in which the means of production are owned by the government or collectively owned.

tragedy of the commons A phenomenon in which competitive pressures cause an unowned resource to be overused and destroyed.

War on Drugs The American policy of criminalizing and punishing the sale and enjoyment of recreational drugs.

War on Terror An umbrella term for interventionist American domestic and foreign policy in the attempt to eradicate and defeat terrorists around the world.

welfare state A government that provides grants, subsidies, training programs, unemployment insurance, health care, and other similar services to the poor.

welfarism The view that part of what justifies political institutions is that they contribute to people's well-being.

zero-sum game A game in which one person can win only to the extent that others lose; an interaction in which one person is made better off only to the extent that others are made worse off.

SUGGESTIONS FOR FURTHER READING

Introductions to Libertarianism for a Popular Audience

Boaz, David. 1998. *Libertarianism: A Primer*. New York: Free Press.

Boaz, David. 1998. *The Libertarian Reader*. New York: Free Press.

Gillespie, Nick, and Matt Welch. 2011. *The Declaration of Independents: How Libertarian Politics Can Fix What's Wrong with America*. New York: Public Affairs.

Huebert, Jacob H. 2010. *Libertarianism Today*. New York: Praeger.

Murray, Charles. 1997. *What It Means to Be a Libertarian*. New York: Broadway.

Economics for a Popular Audience

Friedman, Milton. 2002. *Capitalism and Freedom: 40th Anniversary Edition*. Chicago: University of Chicago Press.

Friedman, Milton, and Rose Friedman. 1990. *Free to Choose: A Personal Statement*. New York: Mariner Books.

Hazlitt, Henry. 1998. *Economics in One Lesson*. New York: Three Rivers Press.

O'Rourke, P. J. 1999. *Eat the Rich*. New York: Atlantic Press.

Roberts, Russ. 2006. *The Choice: A Parable of Free Trade and Protectionism*. New York: Prentice Hall.

Roberts, Russ. 2009. *The Price of Everything*. Princeton, NJ: Princeton University Press.

Sowell, Thomas. 2010. *Basic Economics: A Commonsense Guide to the Economy*. New York: Basic Books.

Classical Liberalism

Bastiat, Frédéric. 1995. "What Is Seen and What Is Unseen," in idem, *Selected Essays on Political Economy*, trans. Seymour Cain, ed. George B. de Huszar. Irvington-on-Hudson, NY: Foundation for Economic Education.

Berlin, Isaiah. 1997. "Two Concepts of Liberty," in idem, *The Proper Study of Mankind*. New York: Farrar, Straus, Giroux.

Buchanan, James. 1975. *The Limits of Liberty: Between Anarchy and Leviathan*. Chicago: University of Chicago Press.

Epstein, Richard. 2004. *Skepticism and Freedom: A Modern Case for Classical Liberalism*. Chicago: University of Chicago Press.

Hayek, F. A. 1978. *The Constitution of Liberty*. Chicago: University of Chicago Press.

Hayek, F. A. 1991. *The Fatal Conceit: The Errors of Socialism*. Chicago: University of Chicago Press.

Locke, John. 1980. *The Second Treatise of Civil Government*. Indianapolis: Hackett Publishing.

Mill, John Stuart. 1978. *On Liberty*. Indianapolis: Hackett Publishing.

Smith, Adam. 2008. *An Inquiry into the Wealth of Nations*. New York: Oxford University Press.

Hard Libertarianism

Lomasky, Loren. 1990. *Persons, Rights, and the Moral Community*. New York: Oxford University Press.

Narveson, Jan. 1988. *The Libertarian Idea*. Philadelphia: Temple University Press.

Nozick, Robert. 1974. *Anarchy, State, and Utopia*. New York: Basic Books.

Paterson, Isabel. 1943. *The God of the Machine*. Edison, NJ: Transaction Publishers.

Rand, Ayn. 1999. *Atlas Shrugged*. New York: Plume.

Neoclassical Liberalism

Brennan, Jason, and John Tomasi. 2012. "Neoclassical Liberalism," in *The Oxford Handbook of Political Philosophy*, ed. David Estlund. New York: Oxford University Press.

Gaus, Gerald F. 1997. *Justificatory Liberalism*. New York: Oxford University Press.

Gaus, Gerald F. 2011. *The Order of Public Reason*. New York: Cambridge University Press.

Schmidtz, David. 1995. *Rational Choice and Moral Agency*. Princeton, NJ: Princeton University Press.

Schmidtz, David. 2006. *Elements of Justice*. New York: Cambridge University Press.

Schmidtz, David. 2008. *Person, Polis, Planet*. New York: Oxford University Press.

Schmidtz, David, and Jason Brennan. 2010. *A Brief History of Liberty*. Oxford: Wiley-Blackwell.

Tomasi, John. 2012. *Free Market Fairness*. Princeton, NJ: Princeton University Press.

Critiques of Libertarianism

Cohen, G. A. 1995. *Self-Ownership, Freedom, and Equality*. New York: Cambridge University Press.

Frank, Robert H. 2011. *The Darwin Economy*. Princeton, NJ: Princeton University Press.

Hudson, William. 2007. *The Libertarian Illusion: Ideology, Public Policy, and the Assault on the Common Good*. New York: CQ Press.

Murphy, Liam, and Thomas Nagel. 2004. *The Myth of Ownership*. New York: Oxford University Press.

Sunstein, Cass, and Stephen Holmes. 2000. *The Cost of Rights*. New York: W. W. Norton and Company.

Government Failure and Public Choice Economics

Easterly, William. 2007. *The White Man's Burden: Why the West Efforts to Aid the Rest Have Done So Much Ill and So Little Good*. New York: Penguin.

Klein, Daniel. 2012. *Knowledge and Coordination: A Liberal Interpretation.* New York: Oxford University Press.

Mueller, Dennis. 2003. *Public Choice III.* New York: Cambridge University Press.

Simmons, Randy. 2011. *Beyond Politics: The Roots of Government Failure.* Washington, DC: Independent Institute.

Tullock, Gordon, Arthur Seldon, and Gordon L. Brady. 2002. *Government Failure: A Primer in Public Choice.* Washington, DC: CATO Institute.

Democracy and Voter Incompetence

Althaus, Scott. 2003. *Collective Preferences in Democratic Politics.* New York: Cambridge University Press.

Brennan, Jason. 2011. *The Ethics of Voting.* Princeton, NJ: Princeton University Press.

Brennan, Jason. 2012. "Political Liberty: Who Needs It?" *Social Philosophy and Policy* 29: 1–27.

Caplan, Bryan. 2008. *The Myth of the Rational Voter: Why Democracies Choose Bad Policies.* Princeton, NJ: Princeton University Press.

Pincione, Guido, and Fernando Tesón. 2011. *Rational Choice and Democratic Deliberation: A Theory of Discourse Failure.* New York: Cambridge University Press.

Markets, Culture, and Civil Society

Beito, David, Peter Gordon, and Alexander Tabarrok. 2009. *The Voluntary City.* Washington, DC: Independent Institute.

Brennan, Jason, 2011. "Civic Virtue without Politics," in idem, *The Ethics of Voting.* Princeton, NJ: Princeton University Press.

Brennan, Jason. 2012. "For-Profit Business as Civic Virtue." *Journal of Business Ethics* 106: 313–324.

Clark, Gregory. 2008. *A Farewell to Alms.* Princeton, NJ: Princeton University Press.

Cowen, Tyler. 2000. *In Praise of Commercial Culture.* Cambridge, MA: Harvard University Press.

Cowen, Tyler. 2004. *Creative Destruction: How Globalization Is Changing the World's Cultures.* Princeton, NJ: Princeton University Press.

McCloskey, Deirdre. 2007. *Bourgeois Virtues: Ethics for an Age of Commerce.* Chicago: University of Chicago Press.

McCloskey, Deirdre. 2011. *Bourgeois Dignity: Why Economics Can't Explain the Modern World.* Chicago: University of Chicago Press.

Rasmussen, Dennis C. 2008. *The Problems and Promise of Commercial Society: Adam Smith's Response to Rousseau,* University Park: Pennsylvania State University Press.

Zak, Paul. 2008. *Moral Markets.* Princeton, NJ: Princeton University Press.

The Welfare State and Poverty

Beito, Charles. 1999. *From Mutual Aid to the Welfare State: Fraternal Societies and Social Services, 1890–1967.* Chapel Hill: University of North Carolina Press.

Cochrane, John H. 2009. "Health-Status Insurance: How Markets Can Provide Health Security." *Policy Analysis,* no. 633.

Murray, Charles. 1984. *Losing Ground: American Social Policy, 1950–1980.* New York: Basic Books.

Murray, Charles. 2006. *In Our Hands: A Plan to Replace the Welfare State.*

Schmidtz, David, and Robert Goodin. 1998. *Social Welfare and Individual Responsibility: For and Against.* New York: Cambridge University Press.

Shapiro, Daniel. 2007. *Is the Welfare State Justified?* New York: Cambridge University Press.

The Warfare State and Nationalism

De Soto, Hernando. 2002. *The Other Path: The Economic Answer to Terrorism.* New York: Basic Books.

Hayek, F. A. 2007. *The Road to Serfdom.* London: Routledge.

Higgs, Robert. 1989. *Crisis and Leviathan: Critical Episodes in the Growth of American Government.* New York: Oxford University Press.

Higgs, Robert. 2004. *Against Leviathan: Government Power and a Free Society*. Washington, DC: Independent Institute.

Kukathas, Chandran. 2007. *The Liberal Archipelago: A Theory of Diversity and Freedom*. New York: Oxford University Press.

Libertarian Anarchism

Chartier, Gary. 2011. *The Conscience of an Anarchist*. New York: Cobden.

Friedman, David. 1989. *The Machinery of Freedom*. New York: Open Court Publishing.

Leeson, Peter. 2014. *Anarchy Unbound: Why Self-Governance Works Better than You Think*. New York: Cambridge University Press.

Rothbard, Murray. 1973. *For a New Liberty: The Libertarian Manifesto*. New York: MacMillan.

Spooner, Lysander. 2010. *No Treason: The Constitution of No Authority*. New York: Kessinger Publishing.

Zywicki, Todd. 2003. "The Rise and Fall of Efficiency in the Common Law: A Supply-Side Analysis." *Northwestern Law Review* 97: 1551–1634.

Libertarian Feminism

McElroy, Wendy. 2002. *Liberty for Women: Freedom and Feminism in the 21st Century*. New York: Ivan R. Dee.

Mill, John Stuart. 1997. *The Subjection of Women*. Mineola, NY: Dover Thrift Editions.

Taylor, Joan Kennedy. 1992. *Reclaiming the Mainstream: Individualist Feminism Rediscovered*. New York: Prometheus Books.

Wollstonecraft, Mary. 2009. *A Vindication of the Rights of Women and a Vindication of the Rights of Man*. New York: Oxford University Press.

Civil Liberties

Bernstein, David E. 2001. *Only One Place of Redress: African Americans, Labor Regulations, and the Courts from the Reconstruction to the New Deal*. Durham, NC: Duke University Press.

Clemens, Michael. 2011. "Economics and Immigration: Trillion Dollar Bills on the Sidewalk?" *Journal of Economic Perspectives* 25: 83–106.

Cohen, Andrew Jason. 2007. "What the Liberal State Should Tolerate within Its Borders." *Canadian Journal of Philosophy* 37: 479–513.

Gray, James. 2001. *Why Our Drug Laws Have Failed: A Judicial Indictment.* Philadelphia: Temple University Press.

Huemer, Michael. 2010. "Is There a Right to Immigrate?" *Social Theory and Practice* 36: 429–461.

Levy, Jacob. 2000. *The Multiculturalism of Fear.* New York: Oxford University Press.

Mill, John Stuart. 1978. *On Liberty.* Indianapolis: Hackett Publishing.

Miron, Jeffrey. 2004. *Drug War Crimes: The Consequences of Prohibition.* Washington, DC: Independent Institute.

Roback, Jennifer. 1984. "Southern Labor Law in the Jim Crow Era: Exploitative or Competitive?" *University of Chicago Law Review* 51: 1161–1192.

Roback, Jennifer. 1986. "The Political Economy of Segregation: The Case of Segregated Streetcars." *Journal of Economic History* 46: 893–917.

Taylor, James Stacey. 2005. *Stakes and Kidneys: Why Markets in Human Body Parts Are Morally Imperative.* Surrey: Ashgate.

Economic Freedom

Bhagwati, Jagdish. 2007. *In Defense of Globalization.* New York: Oxford University Press.

De Soto, Hernando. 2000. *The Mystery of Capital: Why Capitalism Triumphs in the West and Fails Everywhere Else.* New York: Basic Books.

Mises, Ludwig von. 1981. *Socialism.* Indianapolis: Liberty Fund.

Meltzer, Allan H. 2012. *Why Capitalism?* New York: Oxford University Press.

Norberg, Johan. 1997. *In Defense of Global Capitalism.* Stockholm: Timbro.

Pennington, Mark. 2011. *Robust Political Economy.* Northhampton, MA: Edward Elgar Publishing.

Ridley, Matt. 2011. *The Rational Optimist: How Prosperity Evolves.* New York: Harper.

Rosenberg, Nathan, and L. E. Birdzell, Jr. 1987. *How the West Grew Rich*. New York: Basic Books.

Sandefur, Timothy. 2010. *The Right to Earn a Living*. Washington, DC: Cato Institute.

Schmidtz, David, and Jason Brennan. 2010. *A Brief History of Liberty*. Oxford: Wiley-Blackwell.

Tesón, Fernando. 2012. "Why Free Trade Is Required by Justice." *Social Philosophy and Policy* 29: 126–153.

Tomasi, John. 2012. *Free Market Fairness*. Princeton, NJ: Princeton University Press.

Zwolinski, Matthew. 2007. "Sweatshops, Choice, and Exploitation." *Business Ethics Quarterly* 17: 689–727.

Blogs

Asymmetrical Information: www.theatlantic.com/megan-mcardle

Becker-Posner Blog: www.becker-posner-blog.com

Bleeding Heart Libertarians: www.bleedingheartlibertarians.com

Café Hayek: cafehayek.com

EconLog: econlog.econlib.org

The Grumpy Economist: johncochrane.blogspot.com

Hit and Run: reason.com/blog

Ideas: davidfriedman.blogspot.com

Marginal Revolution: www.marginalrevolution.com

The Money Illusion: www.themoneyillusion.com

Overcoming Bias: overcomingbias.org

INDEX